CLEARLY OUTSTANDING

A practical guide to creating outstanding
practice in Early Years Settings

REBECCA MILLER

bookshaker

First Published in Great Britain 2012

by www.BookShaker.com

© Copyright Rebecca Miller

PRAISE

To become 'outstanding' in any walk of life is a long journey that requires commitment, dedication, knowledge and experience.

No one is born an outstanding human being and no team achieves outstanding status on the day that it is formed. There are many elements that have to come together to make an effective team, some that are easy to put in place and some that take time and clear understanding to put into place.

In this book, Rebecca has provided a wealth of ideas for managers and leaders who are striving for excellence within their team. There is no single approach to team leadership that will suit every team leader and by reading *Clearly Outstanding* you will have the opportunity to learn, reflect on and put into place strategies that will engage and improve the setting you are working in.

Although the journey towards outstanding practice can be frustrating at times, it is always worth taking as clearly outstanding practice from adults results in clearly outstanding provision for children.

Alistair Bryce Clegg, author and consultant
www.abcdoes.com

In my role as Nursery Manager, within a busy full day care nursery in Essex, I have known Rebecca in her professional role as Children Centre Teacher for many years. Her expertise, knowledge and enthusiasm throughout was inspiring not only to me but to all those around her. Rebecca has a way of making any concept simple to understand and to then act upon, giving full ownership to every participant as they take changes and actions on board. Thank you for all you have done.

Gill Smith, Nursery Owner

To be a successful leader and manager you need to know where you want to go, what your goals are and how to achieve those goals, inspiring others along the way to share your vision. This is not something that can be easily taught but success hinges upon the effectiveness of it. Yet in Early Years few managers have the opportunity or devote the time to develop their understanding, knowledge and skills in Leadership and Management. Rebecca has been a colleague and friend of mine over the past six years and I have been privileged to be involved in her work on leadership and management in several nurseries and Children's Centres in Tendring. She has provided inspirational Leadership and Management workshops for managers and practitioners, conducted professional dialogues with individuals and worked alongside managers and room leaders to develop and become effective leaders. Rebecca provides the tools and strategies without giving the answers, which ultimately ensures that you have ownership of your own success and you develop in a manner that is natural to your style. I only wish I had known her when I was a head teacher of a primary school, as I am sure that I would have gained so much from her knowledge and wisdom and become a more effective leader and manager.

Ann Tingey, Early Years Advisor

Rebecca has provided specific training tailored to meet the unique needs of the nursery, taking into account the differences in approach by some team members and creating a more unified team vision and ethos. Her warmth, perception and sense of humour has ensured that she inspires others to be the best they can be which has made a tremendous difference to the working environment and quality of the provision we provide.

I and other members of my leadership team also attended a series of Leadership and Management workshops devised and run by Rebecca. These workshops allowed a broad range of managers to really reflect on what constitutes good leadership, to clarify their individual vision and to learn new theories and techniques in order to improve performance. Rebecca's approach was to provide the framework to identify key issues that create difficulties within settings with practical tools and contextual examples of how to overcome them.

Staff felt very energised and inspired by these workshops and the impact has been tremendous both on my own managerial style and the staff's confidence in identifying for themselves any barriers and being proactive in developing and using the right skills to improve team work and productivity. I cannot recommend her highly enough.

Carol Beeson, Nursery Manager, Noahs Nursery

After consultation with our linked day care settings and Children Centre Teachers, Rebecca devised a series of workshops to support the Leadership and Management topics raised by the nursery owners and managers. Her two day course on exploring Leadership and Management, exploring areas such as communication, delegation, appraisals, tackling difficult conversations and creating a clear vision and structure were very successful and have had a very positive impact on the settings. Rebecca also devised workshops to support nursery setting room leaders. Rebecca's professionalism, skill and approach made the workshops both highly informative and fun.

All settings have reported a positive and ongoing impact in improved team work and practice.

I would not hesitate to use Rebecca's services again and would highly recommend her.

Benjamin Mann, Area Manager for Tendring Sure Start Children Centre Services

For Lizzie, my wonderful friend and mentor.
Thank you for believing in me.

CONTENTS

ACKNOWLEDGEMENTS

I FIRST GOT THE IDEA for writing this book following some workshops I planned for the nursery settings I worked with as part of the Sure Start Programme. Without them and the wonderful working relationships I had with the managers and staff, this book would not have been possible.

I would like to particularly thank the managers: Gill Smith, Denise Hawke , Carol Beeson, Carol Thornton-Jones and Ann Williams, Brenda Dearsley and Caroline Allen and all their staff at Little Pals; Chestnut Grove Kindergarten; Noah's Nursery; Pebbles Kindergarten; Willow Tree Nursery; and Oaklea Montessori and all their staff. All of these nurseries, without exception, are fantastic examples of the dedication, care and enthusiasm to provide better opportunities for the children and families in their communities and are doing, in my view, a clearly outstanding job.

A huge thank you to Benjamin Mann, the Area Director of Tendring Sure Start, for his support, faith and encouragement and for giving me the opportunity to develop the workshops.

Thanks, too, to Alan Haylock for all his advice, guidance and support when I was in the nursery settings; his enthusiasm and business knowledge are truly invaluable. Also thanks to Jacqui Burke of Flourishing People for her insight and support.

Thank you to all at Bookshaker and particularly to Lucy, whose support, guidance and infinite patience has propelled me to becoming a better writer.

Last, but by no means least, special thanks to the wonderful team I had the privilege and honour to work with as part of the Sure Start Programme: Ann Tingey, Lucy Partridge, Lisa Gridley and Elaine Broome. I learnt so much from each one of you and I could not possibly have written this book without you all giving so freely of your knowledge, skill, guidance, support and never-ending enthusiasm and passion for what you do. You are all truly outstanding.

FOREWORD

SUSTAINABLE CHILDCARE BUSINESSES RELY ON highly committed people who share a passion for delivering outstanding childcare service. But having a passion for childcare isn't enough on its own. These businesses also need to be managed by people who have a high level of business and management capability. And in today's challenging financial climate, this is more than ever the case.

4Children recently found that only 59% of childcare providers feel confident in their business skills. So, by implication, almost 40% of the sector is being managed by people who aren't quite sure how to run a business successfully. With close to half a million people employed in the sector, this places a huge burden of responsibility on those who manage childcare businesses.

The childcare sector probably suffers from a lack of business and management capability more than many other sectors. Many of those who manage childcare businesses started to work in childcare because it fitted in with their personal circumstances, and somehow over the years found themselves running a business with all of the challenges and responsibility that entails. Having drifted into the role, very few have received any of the formalised business and management skills and training that people tend to access when they make a conscious decision to pursue a career in a certain industry.

In the current environment, where local authorities are less able to provide high levels of business support, training and sustainability funding, being able to access cost effective resources in order to help themselves to develop strong business and management skills is essential.

This book offers just that.

The extremely pragmatic style will appeal to the busy childcare setting manager with limited time and a million other priorities to address. Every point is illustrated with examples that any childcare business manager will be able to relate to. Full of useful tips and checklists, it encourages the reader to approach the book in a very active way, rather than as a passive consumer of ideas.

Clearly Outstanding presents the reader with a selection of some of the most widely used and well-recognised business and management tools, techniques and models, with clear explanations about how these can be applied in a childcare context; so, from the generic to the specific. This, I feel sure, will appeal to readers from within the sector who sometimes feel alienated by generic business language and find it difficult to relate to.

Clearly Outstanding encourages the reader to think strategically, to consult widely and to plan thoroughly in order to ensure business success.

If the suggested approaches in this book are followed, this cannot fail to impact positively on the quality of the childcare provision being offered.

"Good business skills can improve the sustainability of childcare businesses which, in turn, can impact on affordability for parents and quality of provision."

The London Councils – 2007

So for childcare businesses who are striving to deliver outstanding childcare provision, building business and management capability is clearly a contributory factor. *Clearly Outstanding* will become a key tool in supporting this aim.

Jacqui Burke
Founder & Managing
Director of Flourishing People Ltd
www.flourishingpeople.co.uk

INTRODUCTION

TWO YEARS AGO, FOLLOWING A teaching career and having established myself as a coach and trainer, I devised and ran some leadership and management workshops for Early Years settings. By Early Years setting, I mean any organisation that offers education and childcare for children aged up to five years that is regulated by the legal requirements of the Early Years Foundations Stage Education Framework. This came about because of work I was doing with Sure Start, the government initiated project aimed at supporting families in all aspects of childcare in some of the most deprived areas of Britain.

My role was to work with Early Years setting owners and managers, supporting them through direct coaching and training in the management of successful settings within those areas of deprivation. The workshops came about as a result of that experience.

Having worked with many Early Years settings, from small groups providing sessional care in a village hall to independent nurseries or larger pre-schools linked to primary schools, it became increasingly clear that while there was never a lack of talent, enthusiasm or dedication, the leadership and management experience, confidence and skills of the setting managers and owners varied hugely.

The workshops were therefore created to help managers establish clarity and vision in their roles and desired outcomes, to enable their setting to become clearly outstanding. Practical and contextual activities, tools and strategies to help with areas such as time management, communication and all aspects of managing performance, were structured using elements of the OSCAR Model from my coaching and training practice. The OSCAR model is a tool that allows people to explore their aims and establish more positive outcomes through establishing:

- Ownership and Options
- Structure and Systems
- Clarity and Commitment
- Awareness and Action
- Responsibility and Results

This model and the wonderful feedback and learning that the workshops helped create, highlighted the awareness that while the structure, running and organisation between settings may be vastly different, they all share the common aim of wanting to provide a service that is truly outstanding and to have that status verified by Ofsted.

To make any changes that are going to have positive impact and remain sustainable, those changes have to begin at the top and be worked down through the setting. External advisors and consultants can initiate change lower down, model good practice, support the setting-up of routines and systems and influence staff positively to raise standards but this is never maintained unless those changes are first initiated and then effectively communicated and monitored by the owners and managers.

The whole purpose of running an Early Years setting is to provide the best possible environment in which children can thrive. The aim is to foster their creativity and self-esteem so that they can develop the knowledge and skills necessary for them to make the best possible choices as they learn and grow. To find a consistent way of doing so while meeting all the legal requirements and expectations is challenging, to say the least, although I constantly see fantastic examples of staff who do just that.

However, managers have frequently expressed the desire to develop further strategies and skills and my purpose is to provide a way for you to reflect clearly on what being *outstanding* means to you and how you want to create and communicate that.

Developing a greater understanding of your own sense of values and beliefs and how you communicate them, is the key to creating lasting change and putting you on the path to being *clearly outstanding*. If the managers and staff are lacking confidence, self-esteem and commitment to learn then it stands to reason that it will be very difficult to foster the same in the minds of the children the settings are seeking to develop.

To overcome some of the most common difficulties faced by owners and managers, this book will introduce you to some other theories, tools and strategies to help you improve your chosen outcomes, such as:

- Working with other decision makers to create a clear vision and goal for the setting;
- Managing the different expectations of parents, Ofsted and other external advisors;
- Reducing the tendency to react and fire-fight;
- Recruiting and retaining the right staff;
- Creating the best possible working and learning environment;
- Having systems in place that really work;
- Creating positive relationships with all stakeholders (anyone who has an interest in the running of the setting);
- Having the confidence to say "no" and remain focused on your vision while remaining open and flexible to external advice, guidance or ideas;
- Having the time to do everything you want to do.

This book aims to provide you with the opportunity to take a step back and really examine what it is you truly want and how to achieve it. Using tools, strategies and the OSCAR cycle, you will be able to clarify what changes you need to make, along with the systems and techniques you can adopt to gain the most positive outcomes; both for yourself as a manager and for your setting as a whole. Case studies and exercises will provide a contextual background along with practical resources that you can adapt and use as you see fit within your setting.

The responsibility of ensuring *outstanding* quality in the care and education you provide for young children is not something to be taken lightly but, without exception, the managers and owners with whom I have worked, combine this responsibility with a wonderful sense of humour and an open approach to learning and developing themselves and their setting to be the best it can be. To quote Clint Eastwood:

"Let's take the work seriously but not ourselves seriously".

My hope is that this book will be both a practical and fun guide as you work through the process of becoming *clearly outstanding*.

1. ESTABLISHING OUTCOMES

Creating your Vision of an *Outstanding Setting* and
Taking Ownership of it

What is an outcome?

PUT VERY SIMPLY, THE WORD *outcome* relates to an end
product or achievement following predetermined goals
and actions. The outcome, or subsequent result,
depends very much on what those actions were and
how closely they match the intended result.

Most settings would agree that their desired
outcome is to achieve an *Outstanding* Ofsted
inspection, yet this can mean very different things to
many different people. I would also go so far to say this
also means different things to different Ofsted
Inspectors.

An outcome is measured against a set of criteria
which is why most settings are reasonably confident
with the expectations placed on them by Ofsted
guidelines and dutifully fulfil the required Self-
evaluation forms and Development and Action plans in
order to be awarded an *outstanding* judgement.

However, any judgement made by Ofsted or any
other external agency, is very subjective. No amount of
criteria and check lists account for individual
interpretation, hence the often confusing volume of

advice and guidance offered. I don't believe there is any other business in the country that has been subjected to so many changes in such a short period of time.

Most importantly, these changes are imposed following research by and recommendations of various experts in the field, who are guided by their own knowledge, understanding and experiences and so set their expectations as the benchmark for judging good practice across the board.

It is little wonder then, that any Early Years setting is constantly being challenged to justify their practice and produce good results, when the criteria for defining good and *outstanding* are changed so often. When so much is continually being pointed out as being wrong or not good enough, it is very difficult to stay focussed on what is right. This links directly back to a very clear and strong understanding of your own beliefs and values and what, to you, demonstrates *outstanding* practice.

Given that most settings are not run autonomously, the challenge is to create a clear understanding of what the term *outstanding* means to the individual decision makers and other stakeholders and then formulating the vision, practice and actions that will most closely produce it.

All settings have to follow statutory legislation and guidelines, relating to all aspects of running an educational setting. Added to this is the fact that Early

Years settings also need to run as a business and be sustainable. Advice, imposed changes and new initiatives are constantly being thrown at managers and owners. This can make it very difficult to stay focussed on what they feel is truly important, often leading to conflicting interests.

For example, some decision makers are interested only in the financial sustainability of the setting, while others may care more passionately about the terms and conditions under which the staff work. While the goal of being an *outstanding* setting may be the same for both, these two conflicting interpretations may cause direct conflict in terms of the ideal systems and processes each feel should be in place.

This chapter explores the importance of first gaining clarity about your own vision for your setting and what exactly you, as owner or manager, mean by *outstanding*. The next step is to gain the same clarity from the other key decision makers such as governors or board members who have an equal say not only in how the setting is run but how its vision of being *clearly outstanding* is communicated to others. We will look specifically at how to:

Be clear about creating a Mission Statement and how accurately it reflects what you do;

Gain clarity and specific understanding about what you mean by the word *outstanding* and how this matches the views of the other decision makers;

Case Studies and exercises that illustrate the common pitfalls faced by some settings, with strategies to help bring together the views, expectations, roles and responsibilities of the diverse people responsible for what your setting does and how it is viewed by others.

By the end of the chapter you will have had the opportunity to explore where the responsibility for ownership lies, identified what changes may need to be made and what options you have in taking the next step. You will find resources at the end of the chapter that will help you. Using the *As If* and *Disney* strategies with specific examples and a description of how one manager used a simple coaching format, the GROW model, to identify her vision of an ideal setting.

What is your vision? Taking Ownership

Vision is a word that is frequently seen in all manner of contexts across a vast range of establishments. The Vision or Mission Statement, proudly displayed in as many places as possible, is used to capture what is felt to be the essence of an establishment; its purpose, aims and goals.

Here are some examples:
- 'Nurturing, understanding and achievement' (Little Berries Pre-School, Southampton)

- "To help the child to help himself" Maria Montessori (Oaklea Montessori, Dedham)
- 'We nurture, they grow' (Noahs Nursery, Harwich)
- ..."to provide top quality childcare accessible to every child in the area." (Pebbles Kindergarten, Clacton as part of whole statement)

What do those statements mean to you? Do you have a clear picture of what they are about and have you used or seen similar statements yourself? If so, how confident are you that what you do, accurately reflects the vision the statement implies?

The purpose of having a vision statement is to reflect the positive views of everyone who is part of an establishment and communicate its aims and purpose to the wider world. However, the reality is often that the vision has been created by people far removed from the day to day running of an Early Years Setting, such as external Board Directors. In such cases, many of the people to whom the vision refers are unaware of what it says, let alone what it really means, and would be hard pushed to claim enthusiastic allegiance to it.

So if the aim is to have a vision that reflects your personal view of being *outstanding*, are you clear on what that word really means to you?

The meaning of *Outstanding*

The word *outstanding* carries very different meanings for different people. For example:

The *Cambridge Dictionary* definition is:

"excellent; clearly very much better than what is usual"

This definition might seem clear enough for most people, but in terms of an Early Years setting it only works if it is applied to a set of defined and universally understood criteria.

Ofsted would argue that this is indeed the case, defining *outstanding* as, according to their very specific criteria:

'Exceeding expectations'; excellent.

The following descriptor is specifically used as part of the Ofsted report, which highlights the key inspection judgments and what they mean. It describes *outstanding* as: "the provision is of exceptionally high quality".

However, despite very specific guidelines and expectations laid down by the Early Years Foundation Framework those expectations are open to interpretation. The criteria may be set down in black and white but given the huge variety of Early Years settings and the unique needs of the families and communities they serve, one size most definitely does not fit all.

Let's take a look at some of the interpretations of *outstanding* according to the views of different people associated with a wide range of Early Years settings. These comments come from staff, children, inspectors, managers, board directors, advisors and, of course, children:

- My child is safe, happy and well cared for (parent)
- My setting is a centre of excellence (Owner/manager)
- The setting is financially sustainable and we have a long waiting list (Finance Director)
- We work well together as a team and put the children's needs first (Staff member)
- The setting demonstrates *outstanding* practice and leads through a well-structured and thorough system of management (Ofsted)
- I love playing outside (child)

These are just a few random samples; I am sure you will have heard a lot more but all along similar lines. However, what is missing here are the specifics that would actually add meaning to any of the above statements.

For example:

- How exactly is the child happy and safe? What do they experience on a daily basis?
- What specifically makes the setting a centre of excellence? According to whom and to what criteria?
- How is it financially sustainable? Is this the case because you have a minimum staff to child ratio and lots of support through grants and other funding? Are the staff all happy and well-motivated as a result?
- How exactly does the team work together? Does everyone agree with that statement and is that reflected in the atmosphere and positive attitudes evident in the setting?
- What are the specifics of the leadership and management regime that make it *outstanding*? Is this opinion drawn from statements from the Self Evaluation Form and backed by evidence from staff, parents and other stakeholders?
- Does the child enjoy playing outside because it is a regular part of their daily routine or is it because they happen to have been asked on a day when it was a rare treat?

One of the fundamental presuppositions of Neuro Linguistic Programming (NLP) is that everyone responds to their own unique and individual map of the world held in their head. We process billions of bits of information per second, most of which, thankfully we filter out. This filtration process is strongly influenced by our memories, experiences, values and beliefs. Our social and cultural background also influences what we allow in.

For example, imagine a Victorian schoolmaster being transported into a modern nursery. What kind of culture shock do you think he might experience at the sight of children not only being seen and heard but positively encouraged to have their own voice?

While this may be an extreme example, the premise is the same when you take a group of people involved in the running of a child-care setting. They may share a common aim and belief in the importance of providing quality care for children (one would hope) but the range of ages, experiences, beliefs and backgrounds means that they may all have a very different interpretation and approach.

A successful setting therefore must try and recognise these different perspectives and unite them to a common goal or purpose. Not only that, but the setting must have a very clear understanding of the different criteria those individuals are using and what exactly they each expect to see, feel and experience to enable them to recognise and accept it.

To establish a very clear picture of what your vision of an *outstanding* setting is, it is first essential to be proactive in examining the values, beliefs and fundamental reasons behind what guides your actions. Then, in determining your desired end-result, you are more able to act with awareness and intent rather than with a continuous knee-jerk response to and the pressure of, external opinions of what that end-result should be.

Managing Expectations

I have talked with many managers who describe their frustration at being so overwhelmed with information, expectations and sometimes conflicting demands; they feel trapped in the repetition of behaviour and actions that increasingly contradict the values and beliefs they hold and the positive outcomes they are striving to create.

They feel they are being driven more by the expectations of others than their own values, beliefs and personal definition of *outstanding*. This may include a feeling of being bogged-down with dealing with day to day pressures and problems, which impacts on their ability to focus on what they really want to do and achieve. A common result of this is the tendency to feel lost in the problem solving and blame-frame-cycle that leads to confusion and fire-fighting rather than having the time and systems to create solutions and positive outcomes.

It is the process that is important here. Keeping in mind the end-result or outcome requires focus and flexibility; it is, all too often, easy to become over involved in the little details and the worry of being seen to have an obvious end-product that can be evidenced through paperwork.

The following Case Study illustrates this:
In discussion with one Nursery Manager, she explained the outcomes of a recent Board meeting. The Board had unanimously decided that while the nursery was doing well in terms of financial sustainability and capacity and had received a favourable Ofsted Judgement, the next goal was to be awarded the status of *Outstanding*.

The Finance Director had then commented that that specific goal was obviously inherent in everything they did and was the sole aim of the manager at all times.

This was lovely validation for the manager but what was missing was any further specifics about what could actually be done to make any identified improvements, which specifics were responsible for which actions and what role, if any, each director was going to take to support that goal.

Subsequent meetings indicated that all of the Board had varying levels of time available to contribute, experience in the specifics of running a nursery, understanding of the experience or skills they could bring. Most importantly, there was no clear joint understanding of what the word *outstanding* meant to each of them or how they each saw the nursery moving towards it.

This has resulted in frustration on the part of the manager who feels unclear about her specific role and responsibility as well as misunderstanding and miscommunication among the board, which is actually impeding their aim to achieve *outstanding* status.

All members of this board, without exception, have the best interests of the nursery at heart. However, their understanding of and expectations of the purpose of the nursery and what, to them, constitutes being *outstanding*, has not yet been clearly defined.

This lack of clarity dramatically affects everyone's understanding; who has ultimate ownership, what is each person's role, and what is the associated level of influence in determining the options for how the nursery is structured? This then affects the systems that support it, the clarity of the nursery's aims to parents and staff, the lines of communication used and the impact on staff.

Where to start? Establishing your individual Beliefs and Values

When exploring what is important to you and what your individual interpretation of *outstanding* is, it is important to create your views by stating them in the positive and feeling confident that what you are saying accurately reflects your true beliefs, values and priorities. If you are not absolutely clear at this stage then how can you confidently express yourself to others who are also placing a judgement on your setting?

For example, if we look at a statement you may make such as:

- "We are a centre of excellence for quality care and learning." Consider the following questions:
- What, specifically, does that mean to you?
- Who else considers you to be excellent?
- On what basis and criteria are you making that judgement?
- Are you excellent because you are a sustainable business or because of the quality you provide based on feedback from parents, happy and confident children or happy and well-motivated staff?

As you consider the above questions, are you beginning to get a picture in your mind about how your setting looks, sounds and feels? This may sound a little whimsical but to be really clear about what is important to you, it should feel right. When something feels right, it is generally working well.

When it doesn't feel right, you are identifying obstacles and issues that are holding you back and creating negative patterns of thoughts and behaviour that will then impact on everyone else in the setting, creating frustrations such as the ones listed earlier.

Therefore, at this stage, it is important to hold back on any of the potential problems and obstacles that may surface and concentrate solely on the best possible imagined outcome that fits your ideal view of what being *clearly outstanding* means to you.

Exercise to establish your unique vision

On a sheet of paper, write down everything you can think of that matches your ideal interpretation of *outstanding*. Take into account:

* Things that already reflect this in your setting;
* Examples of good practice you may have seen elsewhere;
* Specific examples of what your ideal would be in terms of environment, staff, financing, children, families, other partnership agencies, Ofsted;
* How they already view you and how you would like them to view you;

Write freely, using whatever adjectives and descriptors you like that come to mind. Don't allow yourself to be restricted by negative thoughts or "yes, but..." points; you are writing your ideals and expressing the things that truly matter to you as a person, manager, educator and service provider.

When you have finished, look at what you have written and then list everything in order of priority. Now consider:

- What is absolutely essential to you?
- What other items on your list do you feel strongly about and matter the most to you?
- How much of that is already in place within your setting?

Now that you have a priority list that accurately reflects your beliefs and values, you have a starting point from which to begin the identification of the next steps. Staying with the picture in mind that this is your ideal, begin to identify the specifics of what would need to be seen, heard or felt in order for those beliefs and values to be clearly evident in your *outstanding* setting. For example, imagining that money is no object, consider:

- What environment would you create?
- What would the children be experiencing on a day to day basis?
- What qualities would you have in your staff and how many would there be?
- What systems would be in place to support your ideals?

- How, specifically would you be dealing with outside agencies?
- What resources would you provide?
- How would you be managing your time effectively?
- What would the ideal atmosphere be?

Of course, reality may now be creeping in with an insistent knock on the head. But the point here is that without having the reflective time and clarity to understand what is truly important to you and to have the ideal vision firmly in mind, it is all too easy to get lost in the day to day problems, frustrations and issues inherent in running a setting. This is your opportunity to explore what you feel passionate about and what you are committed to creating in your unique setting.

Who else has a say?

Once you are clear on your own thoughts and ideas, you can now consider the views and opinions of others:

- Who else has a say?
- Do they agree with you?
- What is their interpretation of *outstanding*?
- What do they see as the desired end result?
- What are their priorities?
- What are the identified common goals and what needs to be discussed with a view to finding

solutions and compromise? How do you know and how can you find out?

We have already identified that Ofsted and other partnership agencies or authorities with whom you work will have very specific criteria for their understanding and expectation of *outstanding* and there are obviously very specific, openly communicated, legal requirements to which you must adhere. You may also have to work closely as part of a community enterprise or charity that will also have very specific aims and expectations.

This will obviously vary from setting to setting but, depending on your individual circumstances, you will need to gather as much information as you can about their opinions, views, legal expectations and priorities for what they feel should be the vision of the setting. For example:

- Meeting with the board members to arrive at a unified agreement and approach;
- Holding a planned staff meeting or day to gain the opinions of your staff and to also consider the opinions already expressed by parents and children;
- Using questionnaires to gather evidence or inviting an external advisor or moderator in, to ask on your behalf and gather evidence from an impartial view point;

- Liaison with external agencies to be sure of your legal requirements and expectations to more clearly identify any changes you may need to make.

The key here is to gain clarity by gathering as much knowledge and information as possible. Once you and the decision makers are clear then it becomes easier to examine your options for communicating your vision. You can then begin to address the current structure, systems, roles and responsibilities shared by you and others and to identify any changes you need to make and to which you must commit.

What to do when conflict of views, opinions and values arises

Once you are very clear about what you feel, think and want, it is entirely another matter to gain successful agreement with others and create a unified vision. Every individual will be approaching the task from their individual view of the world and their priorities may be different from yours.

I have to say that the most successful settings I have worked with are privately owned or run with a minimum number of decision makers, thus reducing the dilution of the setting's ethos and purpose. However, even if your setting does have to involve the decisions of others, it is possible to create a general purpose and goal as long as the overall vision is the same, even if the details may differ and the subsequent roles, responsibilities and actions are the result of compromise.

In some cases, this is more difficult if a manager has inherited the staff or setting, particularly if they have become manager after previously working alongside staff as a colleague. In those cases there is an even greater need to be clear about what you want and to identify some of the barriers you feel are holding you back in creating your ideal and becoming a strong manager and leader.

The following case study will give you an example of this:

Case Study

The manager of a nursery was part of a Board with two other members. Her role was the day to day management of the setting and a second Board member was the Finance Director. The third was a distant member who attended meetings and helped with strategy but had no real experience of child care and no defined role in the setting. The Manager and Finance Director shared an office and frequently argued. Despite having the same intended goal of creating a setting that was a centre of excellence, their respective interpretation of what that meant was vastly different from the other and led to many conflicts.

This conflict created a toxic atmosphere that impacted on every aspect of the setting. Staff would play one off against the other. Each would then undermine the other's decisions and regular arguments would have to be mediated by the third Board member.

As you can imagine, the setting became chaotic in its approach and the day to day issues began to take over at the expense of any positive developments, despite regular support from external agencies and advisors. The setting is *outstanding* in many areas of its practice, a judgement verified by its last Ofsted Inspection, yet the continual lack of clarity, communication and systems resulted in low staff morale, lack of mutual trust and a manager who, despite every good intention, remained in reactive fire-fighting mode rather than the pro-active manager she was striving so hard to be.

Creating the right solution

In this instance, a meeting was held where each board member was asked to express their ideal vision of the setting using the exercises outlined earlier. By removing the pressure of the need to recognise where the problems arose and the need to apportion blame, each person was free to be really honest and state their opinions without judgement or fear of being judged.

The result was that for the most part, all the members were in agreement about what they saw as the vision, needs and priorities for the setting. They also shared an understanding, as the meeting developed, of some of the current successes and barriers to that ideal and were in a much more productive state of mind to examine and agree possible solutions.

By recognising that the only result of holding on to their individual beliefs and values was conflict and confusion for all concerned, they learned to accept each other's different views and use them to create a more realistic picture of their options and what actions were needed to achieve them.

Using differences as a positive

One of the names given to the above strategy is the Disney Strategy, from Walt Disney's famous method of using people's different views as a means to reduce conflict and create more positive outcomes. The process is very simple but requires an open mind and the joint intention to focus on solutions and options rather than proving whose opinion is the most valid.

In broad terms, a group of people responsible for key decisions will fall into the following three categories:

- The role of the killjoy. This is the person who is always negative and always thinks of the potential problems attached to any new idea or initiative.

- The role of the dreamer. This is the idealist, the creative person who may be the driving passion behind creating and sustaining the vision and who constantly looks for new ways to improve things.
- The role of the Realist. This is the person who may share the dreamer's passion but will temper their enthusiasm by pointing out important facts that need to be taken into account in order for their idea to work.

Which one are you? Can you identify which role the other decision makers you work with tend to lean towards?

The tendency may be to stay stuck in these roles and make the differences become personal as the above case study illustrates. Yet, if the differences are recognised as a useful tool to support the common outcome goals for the setting, a much more collaborative approach to making, communicating and sustaining the identified changes can be found.

Examples of when the strategy can be used include:

- Using it as the basis for a Board meeting to determine the common goal and individual roles and responsibilities, as well as the Board's expectations of you;
- When you are trying to reach an agreed specific course of action and are trying to be more creative in your approach;

- When you want to test out a new idea or strategy and gain a different perspective on the possible outcomes or when there is a conflict between opinions and the ideal you are trying to create versus the practicalities of making it happen.

In the above case study, the strategy was used by asking the three members to swap roles and look at the situation specifically from the other's perspective. The Financial Director considered options based on the imagined case of money being no object to meet his expressed ideal outcome. The manager looked at the same situation but with more of a realist perspective, looking specifically for the nuts and bolts and consequences of the different outcomes. The more negative and distant board member took on the role of dreamer and expressed his opinions through his ideal interpretation of being *outstanding*.

Alternatively, if there are more people involved, all members could work together as a group, with the meeting broken down into three separate stages, working through each role as a separate phase to really look at the situation from every conceivable angle.

Introducing change

Once there is clarity about your intended outcomes and vision you must then assess if your setting has the potential to match those values and be successful according to the combined perspective of the relevant decision makers' definition of *outstanding*.

Inevitably, unless these exercises have shown that all the decision makers are in perfect harmony and you are already clearly communicating and evidencing your desired interpretation of being *clearly outstanding*, you will have identified some changes that you need to make.

It is important however, to remember that the likelihood of everyone being in total agreement with every aspect of your vision is nigh on impossible. However, it is absolutely essential that not only you, but the other key decision makers are extremely clear about what it is you are setting out to achieve before you begin to assess how you communicate that vision to others.

The concept of change is always daunting and it is important to consider the potential impact the identified courses of action you are about to take may have before you actually take them. For example, you will need to identify exactly who will be affected by the changes and how; what the likely obstacles are to any changes you want to make; the solutions you can see to help overcome them and where or to whom you can go for support and guidance.

There are many consultants and advisors available that will appeal to you and your vision of what *outstanding* practice looks like. Take the time to look for them and gather their input as well as identify any other places where you have seen similar practice, changes or outcomes that work successfully. You are then in a far stronger position to identify the specific actions that have made them – and could now make you – more successful.

Identifying potential obstacles at this stage will enable you to be clear in how you form your strategy and involve everyone in the change process.

To do this you need to effectively consider and take on board the opinions and views of others in the setting and establish the necessary next steps to ensure that any changes you do make are positive, consistent, clearly communicated and sustainable.

Gathering the input of others

There are many ways you may choose to do this but the following form some of the most common and successful strategies I have seen employed:

- Give staff a guided exercise similar to the one you completed in order for them to reflect upon what the word *outstanding* means to them and how it is currently matched in the setting;
- Use the exercise as the basis for a planned whole staff day so that all views can be expressed and an agreed common definition reached;
- In light of this, systematically examine your current systems and practice. This will include

reviewing how staff are currently recruited, trained and developed, the frequency and effectiveness of staff meetings and appraisals and any other ways that lines of communication are established and monitored;

- Identify any areas that require developing and any changes you wish to make.

- Once identified, use these as the basis for creating specific, measurable and actionable steps that are clearly communicated and monitored. (This may include amending your SEF and current Development Plan);

- Create a realistic time frame and priority list to effect those changes and be crystal clear about who is accountable for which actions and how they will be reviewed.

Summary

This chapter has given you some specific tools and strategies to use in creating clarity within your personal vision and understanding of *outstanding* and how that fits with the clearly expressed views of the other decision makers. By taking ownership, you are now ready to look at what options you have.

You will also have identified any current patterns of thoughts, behaviour and actions that are preventing you from creating and achieving that vision while recognising the value of understanding the different perspectives, knowledge and skills of others.

You will also hopefully now have more confidence in your own beliefs and values and so feel better prepared to create the structure and systems that will support the right environment, staff, skills and behaviour to uphold them. This will also give you the confidence to question any new ideas and initiatives presented to you and not panic yourself and your staff into automatically adopting them when they don't fit your clear vision and desired outcomes.

There is a great deal of value to be had by drawing on the knowledge, skills and experiences of others as well as feeling confident to meet the legal requirements expected of you in terms of quality of care and provision. The aim here is to have absolute clarity about what you feel is truly important and so base your decisions on what you feel is right and not solely on the opinion of others.

The next step is to clarify exactly how you currently communicate and evidence your setting's vision, systems and outcomes. This includes how you communicate with parents, staff, children, external advisors and partnership agencies as well as Ofsted, with the intention of making the necessary changes to ensure that you truly are being *clearly outstanding*.

Questions to help determine Board members' roles and responsibilities and expectations of the manager

Often when there is a Board or charity that is directly responsible for setting outcomes and sustainability, lines of communication regarding roles, responsibilities and expectations can often become blurred. The following is a list of questions that may be useful in helping to determine clarity for your individual setting and circumstances.

- Who is the ultimate decision maker?
- What is their specific role?
- Do they share that responsibility with anyone else?
- What power do they ultimately hold?
- What is the role of the Chairperson?
- Are they a key decision maker or is their role that of a facilitator?
- How many board members are there?
- How often does the board meet and how is the agenda decided upon/
- Who is responsible for communicating meeting dates and agenda?
- What is the role of each board member? Are they there as sounding boards but with no real decision making power? What is their individual interest, knowledge or skill base? How much time can they offer in real terms?

- How are decisions made? What is the process? Is it fair and consistent? What impact does this process have on the manager or others connected with the actual running of the setting?
- What is the designated role of the manager?
- How much decision making power do they possess?
- Who is their line manager?
- Who can they talk to or go to for support and guidance?
- What, specifically, is their role and has this been discussed and agreed as part of a specific job specification?
- How are they expected to report to the Board?
- What specific responsibilities are they expected to have?
- How much day to day input does the Board require?
- How often is the manager's role reviewed?
- What continuous professional development is in place for the manager?
- How often do they have appraisals and who is the best person to conduct them?
- How involved has the Board been in establishing the vision for the setting?
- Do they regularly contribute to the SEF, Development or Action plans?

- How are the main priorities for the setting decided upon?
- Who is responsible for co-ordinating any specific actions?
- What process for reflection is in place?
- Is there a high level of trust between all Board members?
- Is there clarity about who does what, why and when?
- What support systems are in place?

GROW Coaching Model

Goals

Reality

Options

Will

G — Goals: The process of setting the goals, what is desired, using effective questions rather than instructions or commands to raise awareness.

R —Reality: Identifying the current situation and what barriers there are, both external and internal, to achieving those goals.

O — Options: What are you actually going to do? How? How will you know if you are succeeding? What strategies will you have if you face any identified barriers or sudden changes?

W — Will: What is your will to commit? How much effort are you going to take? What are the markers for your success? Can you identify the necessary steps and effort required to move towards your identified goals?

House of Change

This is a useful model to help look at how people progress through a cycle of change in a work setting. It was developed by Paul Kirkbridge and Jim Durcan in the 1990s to communicate to managers the key aspects of personal and organisational change. There are four rooms to the house as shown in the diagram below:

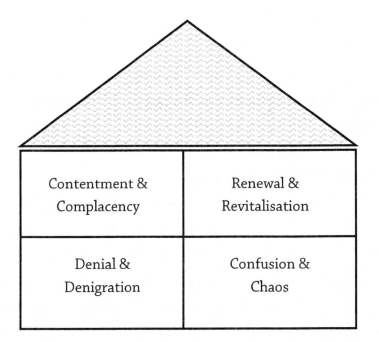

| Contentment & Complacency | Renewal & Revitalisation |
| Denial & Denigration | Confusion & Chaos |

The principles of the model are as follows:

- All organisations and individuals have to go from room to room in an anticlockwise direction.
- Organisations and individuals do not have to spend the same amount of time in each room.
- Organisations will have people in each of the four rooms at any one time.
- There is no end point – one continues travelling round the rooms throughout one's life and career.
- Survival is not compulsory – some individuals and organisations will get stuck and die, usually in Denial.
- To get from Contentment to Renewal, one has to go through Denial and Confusion.
- Renewal and Revitalisation always turns into Contentment and Complacency and often in an instant.

Helping people move through the Change House

1. From contentment to denial – Problem Recognition

- Get people to benchmark. What would successful change look like?
- Provide data/stories on how well other settings are doing and why?
- Get people to go outside the setting and visit others.
- Provide a symbolic shock as in the worst case scenario.

- Provide resistant staff members with a platform to express their views openly and within a structure.

2. Denial to Confusion – Problem Ownership

- Continue benchmarking and external feedback, for example from other settings and advisors.
- Expose the majority of employees to the problem. For example if staff members are disgruntled at not having a pay rise, inform them of the financial reality being faced.
- Avoid providing solutions, ask them to consider and contribute. Staff meetings to focus on the Development plan are good for this.
- Support those looking for solutions. Give praise and acknowledge good ideas wherever possible.
- Get rid of those really stuck in denial. This is tricky, but goes back to being clear about the skills, capabilities and attitudes you expect in your setting.

3. From confusion to renewal – Solution Generation

- Provide vision and a direction. Remember, once you are clear you will be more clear and consistent in how you communicate and create the desired outcomes.
- Sell solutions, don't tell. Involve people as far as possible in the decision making.
- Focus on first steps. Use your Development plans, SMART plans and action plans to demonstrate.
- Set demanding but attainable goals.

- Feedback results quickly and regularly.
- Reward new behaviour/performance by showing appreciation and validation through whatever means you have identified as being successful.

4. Preventing slippage into contentment – Solution Implementation

- Keep focusing on whole and individual performance targets in staff meetings and individual appraisals.
- Keep providing feedback – internal and external.
- Keep refining and transmitting the strategy and vision.
- Celebrate success but always link to new targets/objectives/visions through your SEF and Development plans.

2. COMMUNICATING YOUR VISION

NOW YOU HAVE ESTABLISHED WHAT *outstanding* means to you and gained some clarity and agreement from other decision makers if necessary, it is time to look at exactly how you communicate that understanding to others.

You may have already identified some key areas for change and the focus now is to determine to whom you specifically need to communicate and the key messages that you want them to receive.

This chapter will help you determine the methods you currently use, their effectiveness and any barriers to successful communication that need to be overcome. Case study examples, tips and strategies will enable you to clearly examine your options and commit to the creation of new ways to ensure that you communicate the right messages to parents, children, staff, partnership agencies and external advisors and inspectors.

At the end of this chapter you will find resources to help you identify your current strengths and suggested questions, formats and tips for any changes you wish to make within the context of specific examples.

It is crucial to understand that in communicating your understanding of what *outstanding* practice means to you, the understanding and interpretation of others will be very different according to their unique thoughts, feelings and experiences. Another term for this is criteria and you need to be clear about which criteria your understanding, decisions, behaviour and actions are all based.

Very often, we mistakenly believe and assume that others share our expectation of the behaviour we want to see as evidence of our own criteria being met.

For example, let's say that you highlight the importance of outside play in your setting. For you, this may mean that children have frequent access to a well-resourced and organised outside area within a free-flow system. Your staff may see that as specific play-times outside where children just run about or play on wheeled toys. Parents may not see the point of it at all and be extremely concerned that their child will be forced outside in the cold and come home with unwanted dirty clothes. Ofsted may see that the provision and practice is not allowing enough opportunity for exploration and sustained shared thinking.

We have already established that everyone will have their own unique view of what *outstanding* means to them. However, what this and numerous other examples indicate is that you need to make it explicitly clear what you, as the owner and manager, mean by outdoor play. That way, your systems, expectations and monitoring will more clearly communicate to others.

The sheer volume of expectations from the different people who use and view your setting means that you will have numerous ways of communicating with them. The effectiveness of those means is determined by how those different people then respond and communicate with you. This can be both rewarding and challenging and requires you to be clear, consistent and flexible while always remaining authentic in what you say and do.

Communicating with parents

Parents are, of course, crucial to the success of a setting. They are your customers and it is vital to understand their needs and requirements while also being very clear about what it is, exactly, your setting provides.

Location, finance, community and transport all play a part in how parents choose a setting for their child but most parents will ultimately base their decision on where they feel their child will be most safe and happiest. I am, of course, making a huge assumption here. NLP demonstrates that we can never assume to know exactly how someone else thinks or feels and no matter how hard we try, we are never going to please all of the people all of the time.

The key is to be very clear about the most common needs of the community you serve, while also being flexible enough to provide individual consideration. The aim is to run your setting as a sustainable business while also providing the highest quality care and education as you have now determined that to be. So how do you know if this is what the parents in your area actually want and are you absolutely clear about how you inform and include them in the process?

Evidence of their interest and satisfaction with what you offer, according to their understanding of an *outstanding* setting, may include:

- Their children regularly attend;
- They pay their fees regularly and on time;
- They take an active interest in the setting and become involved with various supportive events;
- They understand and support the practice you offer;
- They maintain close relations with their child's key worker;
- They attend parents information evenings;
- They read and add their thoughts and comments to your Development Plan (the document linked to your Self Evaluation Form);
- They recommend you to other parents;
- They communicate their positive thoughts and feelings through what they say, responses in

questionnaires you have asked them to complete and any other channels of input you have in place in your setting.

If this is the case then you obviously don't need to read any further. If this is not the case and you are regularly dealing with parents who are: late or non-payers, frequently complain about their child coming home with messy or dirty clothes, place restrictions on their child going outside, never engage with you or their child's key worker, frequently complain about the quality of care or service you provide or even remove their children, then part of the reason may be that you are neither communicating clearly enough nor engaging them in appropriate ways to seek their input.

I am very well aware that settings often do their absolute utmost to meet all of the above criteria and still encounter problems with some parents and carers. There are many reasons for this that may have little or nothing to do with how you operate as a setting. However, depending on the number and frequency of any of these issues, it may be worth looking at what you are currently doing to see if there are alternative systems and methods of communication you can put in place to achieve more positive outcomes.

What parents may base their decision on

If we return to the vision you established in chapter one and the specific ways your setting delivers it, what exactly is it that you want parents to see, hear and feel when they come to your setting, so that they can make the most informed choice about whether that is where they are happy to send their child?

Every parent will have different criteria for the choices they make but will invariably wish to be clearly informed of some or all of the following:

- The fees you charge and the structure and options of paying them;
- The accessibility to funded places;
- Ease of access to the setting;
- Wrap around care such as breakfast and after school clubs;
- Provision of hot food and snacks;
- The quality of care in terms of safeguarding and following of the Early Years Foundation Stage requirements;
- The professional and personal qualities and qualifications of your staff;
- The learning environment both inside and out;
- How inclusive you are;
- How well you communicate what you do on a day to day basis;

- How clearly you state and provide access to your policies, SEF and Development Plans;
- How welcoming you are to parents and how much you value their partnership and input;
- The links to the community you serve;
- The provision and signposting to other services parents might need.

These may all seem very obvious and all of the settings I have worked with have had this information available in some form. Information is often presented through written literature such as the setting Self Evaluation Form, Development and Action Plans, Operation Plan, setting policies, parent prospectus, website, display boards, newsletters, posters, photos, digital screens, leaflets and verbal communication with staff and other parents.

However, while all of these may be in place, the effectiveness of how well they are used or accurately reflect the actual practice in a setting may differ. This is often a result of issues such as: lack of confidence felt by the manager or staff, staff turnover resulting in updated information not being shared, lack of time, lack of clarity in what is written, lack of access by both staff and parents to relevant information, lack of interest and too much difference between what is being said and what is actually observed by parents when they come in to the setting.

Another very common issue is lack of consistency. Sometimes with very good intentions, managers may not be consistent in their expectations of or communication with parents which can have wider reaching implications for the setting as the following case study illustrates.

Case Study

I once worked with a setting manager who was faultless in the production and delivery of all the above pieces of literature that arguably left parents in no doubt about what the setting offered and its subsequent expectations from parents.

However, she frequently ran into difficulties in a number of ways. She had many parents who were late payers or simply didn't pay at all. Other parents regularly dropped and picked up their children early or late. Others frequently forgot to provide children with appropriate clothing or snacks as specified in the policy and the manager, in all of these cases, found it very difficult to tackle the issues with the parents.

Can you imagine the subsequent impact on her staff and setting? The accounts were frequently out of balance, staff ratios were continuously interrupted, and other parents became angry and frustrated on hearing that while they paid their fees on time, other parents were allowed special rates or terms. Worse, some parents who were notorious for such behaviour began to introduce other parents who considered the nursery a soft touch. Added to this was the abuse some staff and the manager received when trying to solve these issues, all of which resulted in plummeting staff morale and the faltering of systems.

This manager is by no means alone. The issues may seem small but the impact is huge. The main issue here was that the manager lacked confidence in the systems that were in place as they were at odds with her values and beliefs around how parents should be handled. She also cared deeply for her staff and felt increasingly frustrated at the difficulties in managing their stress and discomfort, as well as the differing demands of the parents, and the systems in place that she felt did not accurately reflect her view of good practice.

The whole purpose of having systems is that they accurately reflect your true intentions, they are clearly communicated to and understood by those who need to access them and that you are consistent in following the processes you have identified within them.

Most people are more than happy to abide by rules and expectations providing they are made clear from the start and the reasons for them are fair and of benefit to all.

Case study

Another setting I know does exactly that. They are an Ofsted awarded *outstanding* setting and it is very easy to see why. The literature and information that they provide about what they do and what they don't do, is crystal clear. Parents are left in absolutely no doubt the reasons for their systems and the consequences if they are not adhered to. Do parents always like it? Of course not. Do they sometimes remove their children? Occasionally.

The vast majority of the parents, though, are very happy with the systems as they were made very aware of them before sending their child to the setting. There were no surprises, no changes in expectations from either side so very few misunderstandings or conflicts. The same applies to the communication of expectations to their staff which we will look more closely at in the following chapter.

Examples of good practice
Your setting prospectus

It is clear, simply written and covers everything a parent would want or need to know. A good prospectus will include your vision, the reason why you do what you say you do and exactly what the parent can expect if they send their child to you. If you are unsure what to include, look at examples of other settings and see how much of what they say matches what is important to you and your setting.

Your website

This should be an extension of your prospectus. It should again be simple and clear with links to important areas of information. Depending on what messages you particularly want to get across, you may have photos showing the children enjoying a range of activities and resources with examples of comments made by the children themselves about what they are doing. You may have links to other partnership agencies or to services that are unique to your setting such as holiday and after school clubs, additional support, special activities or visitors. Continually updated information about your fees, payment methods, opening times and about dropping off and picking up procedures would be useful.

You may also wish to include photos of your staff and highlight their qualifications and particular interests. Think about what makes your setting unique, what is it that you want parents to see, feel and hear if they visit your setting? Once you have identified that, incorporating it into your website will give the most accurate reflection of what actually happens in your setting and gives parents the knowledge to make the most informed choice.

Display boards

There is nothing more off putting than seeing a foyer or display board that is cluttered with lots of written information such as posters and leaflets. Think about what it is you actually want and need parents to know and bear in mind that you may have some parents or carers who may not be confident with reading and will need the information to be accessible in a way that is more comfortable and relevant to them.

Photos will say a thousand words and captions next to them will give the essence of what the children are actually doing and why. There are numerous recording devices that can be attached to displays that when pressed will play a message recorded by either staff or children, which can be very effective.

The Setting Development Plan

I have seen several settings that create a visual display based around their Development Plan. An updated plan is put on display and embellished with appropriate photos, notes and statements from children, staff, parents and other visitors about what is currently going on in the setting and future plans for development. This will include examples of new projects such as the purchasing of new resources, changes to the environment, plans and maps as well as examples of children's work and photos of them at play. Parents are then invited to add their own comments and suggestions. This is also an excellent vehicle for demonstrating how the children's input is also valued in the setting.

Newsletters

Most settings produce these but again the length, content and frequency will vary. It is important again to consider its purpose and if this is the most effective means of communicating key messages to parents. For example, are they always printed and sent home with the children? Are they displayed anywhere else in the nursery? Are they available electronically? Is there an app that can be used so it is downloaded in a verbal format for parents to listen to? What are the key messages you want to give? Does it vary from month to month or week to week?

Your Policies and Procedures

This may well include a separate parent information pack that highlights more specifics such as emergency contact numbers, medicines and allergies and expectations around food, drinks, payment, clothing etc. In short, all your policies are there to inform anyone of exactly what happens in your setting and why.

There are many policy templates available through various Quality Assurance schemes and I have seen settings that have simply taken them and changed the headings to match their individual logo. There is nothing wrong with this in itself as the quality and quantity of these policies are basically very sound. However, the point of having policies and procedures is that they are a reflection of you. They should be unique and include detail that matches your intentions and accurately reflects the values of your individual practice and provision.

Further suggestions

Given the diverse needs and interests of the parents who will be coming to your setting, it is always wise to consider as many different ways of getting your message across as you can.

The above examples all have their place; however, a familiar barrier encountered is that despite best efforts, settings simply cannot get parents to engage in their child's learning.

Some parents are extremely busy and simply don't have the time to stop and talk if they are dropping off or picking up their children and also may find it difficult to attend induction or parents' evenings. Others may not be busy but still find it difficult to engage.

Some further ideas I have come across to help address this problem involve the embracement of technology. Some settings have digital screens in the foyer which regularly show photos, key messages, the setting newsletter and messages from staff. Other settings have taken this one step further to have a Twitter and/or Facebook account that parents can access to receive daily information and updates.

Many parents will have a smart phone, and an app that can be used to download information and data can be extremely effective.

To be unique or to be *outstanding* from your perspective, you need to have your intended outcome and end result always firmly in mind. You are providing a service and you are being extremely clear about what that service is. You are providing parents with knowledge which is then allowing them to make an informed choice. So many settings forget this and get tied up in knots trying to alter what they offer to suit individual parents. While this is both admirable and in fact desirable as part of being flexible and accommodating, it is important to remember that you cannot please all of the people all of the time. Some of your methods and expectations will not suit all parents and some may as a result choose to send their children to another setting.

Being *clearly outstanding* means just that, being clear. There are lots of fantastic examples available of effective ways to communicate to parents and it is in your best interest to seek out advice, support or even visit other settings that will offer you more options in what you can do.

Once you have your methods in place, this is the means by how you will be viewed and judged by others so it is vital that you feel truly happy with your key messages and that you welcome feedback to continually reflect upon and improve your service.

Communicating to staff

We will be looking in more detail at the recruitment and retention of staff in the next chapter. However, being clear and consistent about what you want your staff to know and do is vital in the running of a successful setting.

As in the example with communicating with parents, knowledge is power. The more open, clear and consistent you are about what you do, what you expect and why, the less opportunity there will be for confusion and potential issues due to misunderstanding. What exactly would you like your staff to say about working for you? What, specifically, do you need to communicate to them in terms of roles, responsibilities, attitudes and expectations?

What your staff are likely to say

The easiest way to illustrate this is to look at two case studies from two different settings. Both settings have been awarded *outstanding* in their last Ofsted inspection and so demonstrate very good practice. However, the staff at one setting are consistently positive in their attitude and approach while the staff in the other are less so.

Case study

This setting has an extremely clear and explicit prospectus and policy procedure. It is privately owned and the manager has worked extremely hard to build and maintain its excellent reputation. She has a very specific set of expectations of her staff and these are made extremely clear at interview and then induction stages. Clear job descriptions, regular mentoring and in depth information pack guides a new staff member about what exactly he or she is expected to do, what training and support is available and what the lines of communication are for any areas of concern.

This manager expects staff to attend weekly room meetings as well as other staff meetings and training, some of which is unpaid. The staff, on the whole, are consistently highly motivated, enthusiastic and there are rarely cases of prolonged or frequent absenteeism. This particular setting is regularly visited by other settings as an example of *outstanding* practice.

Case Study

The care and support offered to the children and parents in this setting is considered exemplary. The setting also has very clear and specific policies and guidelines which are communicated to staff and there is also an expectation that staff attend room meetings and other staff meetings and trainings. This is usually paid attendance.

The manager works hard to offer support and guidance to new staff and regularly places them in rooms with more experienced staff.

However, while the care and nurturing are excellent, the manager is frequently frustrated by staff members who are regularly absent or unwilling to attend additional meetings, conflict between rooms and different staff members, and inconsistency in following agreed protocol and procedures.

The atmosphere is not always happy or co-operative and the quality of what is being offered can sometimes suffer as a result.

This particular setting is not privately owned but this isn't the reason for the differences between them.

Very simply it is a matter of expectation. The manager in the first case study is in absolutely no doubt about what her setting is about and how she wants it to run and be perceived by others.

The second manager is equally passionate and committed but had lacked the clarity of an established and agreed vision and ethos that accurately reflected her confidence in creating and delivering the right systems to support it.

Things to put in place

Time and again the root issue is one of clarity and consistency. Once you are clear about what you want and therefore what to expect, you can communicate this so that any staff member either established or new, knows exactly what to expect, what to do and how they will be treated. They will also have absolute trust in your ability to be open and consistent in your management.

The essentials to ensure clear communication and therefore good practice include having:

- Clearly defined job descriptions outlining expected attitudes, behaviour, attendance expectations and performance role and responsibilities;
- A staff handbook explaining all the beliefs, attitudes, knowledge and skills you require. This could also include your training and development programme, mentoring programme and specific training you as an employer will provide to support new and existing staff members to develop their role;
- Clearly written systems to evidence the practice and lines of communication within the setting
- Specific details of when room and staff meetings will take place and whether or not staff attendance is compulsory and in addition to paid working hours;

- Details of what, exactly, staff can expect from you as a manager in terms of time, resources, flexibility and communication;
- The frequency and nature of staff appraisals;
- How staff's individual skills, capabilities, knowledge and ideas will be taken into consideration.

Consulting with children

Consulting with children is always high on the EYFS agenda. Many training initiatives and tool kits have been created to actively take in to account the views of the children to continually improve the services and activities they access.

Essentially, your communication with the children in your care comes directly from the environment you create and the attitudes, skills and dispositions of the staff you employ. An important issue to consider here is exactly how clear is your vision of how an *outstanding* environment actually looks, sounds and feels.

Are you happy with the environment you provide and how well children access and thrive within it? What exactly are the experiences you wish to provide for the children and how can you demonstrate that their views and opinions, from babies upwards, are truly being valued and are reflected in your practice?

With this in mind, consider:

- What methods of observation and recording do you currently use?
- Is it clear that the interests and needs of the children are at the forefront of any systems you have in place?
- How can you show that?
- What do you do to actively encourage children to share their opinions and to demonstrate that these are valued?
- How do you know that your methods and systems are successful?
- Where can you go for further advice or information?
- Is there another setting, advisor or peer that you admire that you would be happy to ask for support and model their methods and systems?
- What will a child see, feel and experience if they come to your setting?

Being clear on this is absolutely essential in helping you have the confidence and authority to work with external agencies and to pass an Ofsted inspection with the judgement you truly want to have. Therefore you need to look at things from the child's point of view and then demonstrate how you have taken this into consideration in a manner that will be clearly evident if an Inspector or Moderator walks into any of your rooms.

For example:

- Are the display boards relevant to the children all at eye level?
- Are they full of the children's work or merely a reflection of the adults' taste?
- Are there lots of photos and comments on the wall demonstrating children's learning and enjoyment, making it very clear about the nature and purpose of the activity they are engaged in?
- Are there comments from the children evidenced on your Development Plan? Does your planning reflect that practitioners have followed the children's individual interests and needs?
- Does the learning environment clearly support and demonstrate how children access and use it?
- Can your staff evidence through their observation notes, planning, room layout, interaction with the children and examples of specific tools to demonstrate that children's input is valued?

Communicating with Ofsted and other External Agencies

Ofsted has a very clear legal framework and set of criteria against which they judge a setting. You will also no doubt be judged by the Local Authority through specific assessment systems that will impact on the amount of funding or access to support and training your setting receives. Some settings actively seek out participation in other Quality Assurance Programmes such as those offered by The Pre-School Learning Alliance or National Day Nursery Association.

One of the key tools used by settings is the Self Evaluation Form (SEF). It is not a legal requirement but it is considered to be an excellent investment of the setting's time to complete as it will specifically evidence all areas of the settings environment, practice and statutory obligations in their provision of care and learning.

Used properly, the SEF is an invaluable reflective tool and is most effective when used to inform the setting's Development and subsequent Action plans. These plans are key in how you communicate what you do and why. They form the most effective means to communicate what you consider to be an *outstanding* practice, through your clearly defined vision, values and beliefs about *outstanding*.

Ofsted will look at your submitted SEF and study it in detail before they visit. When they visit, they will not necessarily be interested in seeing more paperwork evidence but will rather be looking for evidence that supports your SEF statements in the environment and by talking to and observing parents, children and staff.

The criteria Ofsted will then use to judge a setting is very explicit but the person carrying out the inspection is subject to their own interpretation, based on their individual ideas, beliefs and experiences. This is why so many settings complain that they have not been, in their view, awarded full recognition through *outstanding* status.

Again though, how clear are you really being and how consistent are you in setting out the relevant systems and behaviour that support your stated vision? In my experience, when a setting is completing the SEF or other Quality Assessment forms, it is very easy to write the words Ofsted are looking for and be incredibly convincing in what they say they do.

However, if that is not really an accurate reflection of the systems and practice in place then they are vulnerable to imposing more changes that may move them even further away from their interpretation and intention of being *outstanding*.

I have known many managers who write out endless Quality Assessment forms to comply with the requests of various external agencies or partners and then do not communicate this effectively to their staff. The result is often a great deal of confusion and misalignment of what staff have believed to be the setting's intentions. They may then lack the confidence, not only in what they do, but in how they communicate that when external inspectors arrive.

The SEF and any follow up plans represent your opportunity, not only to be absolutely clear and confident in what you intend, but if staff, parents and the children are clearly involved in the process then they are more likely to be confident to reflect that in their practice and then communicate it to others.

Your Development Plan can then be used to identify any current or potential issues and prioritise them in terms of importance. Everyone is involved, everyone is clear and everyone is then more confident to fulfil and communicate the required expectations.

Your attention can then be placed more on how your environment and staff demonstrate your *outstanding* practice. Displays, as before, can clearly demonstrate the nature and purpose of the activities and experiences on offer. Photos and captions will demonstrate the level of interaction between the adults and the children, the quality of the experiences on offer, how the children use the environment and how their voice is clearly heard and used to inform planning and next steps. Your paperwork forms only a small part of what Ofsted will see so you need to be clear, both in what you say and do and demonstrate that in as many ways as possible.

Summary

We have established to whom and why who you need to communicate and how to achieve that communication. By being clear about the messages you want to give, you are more able to find the most effective ways to achieve effective communication so that everyone who comes in to your setting, no matter what their reason or individual perspective, is left in no doubt about your beliefs, values and intentions.

The next chapter will deal more specifically with recruiting the right staff to match your vision of *outstanding* and the best ways of managing and retaining them.

Chapter resources: tips and questions for how to clearly evidence your procedures and systems

The environment

Nothing will reflect *outstanding* practice more than if parents, visitors or Inspectors walk in to your setting and see children happily engaged in a range of activities, a calm atmosphere and staff looking relaxed, confident and happy. Most importantly they will see a high level of interaction.

Yes, you will have folders of evidence, which I urge you to thrust under the noses of Inspectors, although parents may find this a bit off putting and unnecessary. The paperwork is an important part of your evidence but is only useful if it truly reflects what the Inspectors are seeing, hearing and feeling. Some of the best examples I have seen where the environment clearly reflects the *outstanding* practice are:

- A warm and welcoming foyer that is not too bright or cluttered.

- Well placed and thought out displays that serve a particular purpose or are conveying a specific message. For example, properly approved photos of children playing outside and captions describing their own words on what they are doing and how much fun they are having.
- A clearly laid out Development plan highlighting recent projects and successes, evidenced by photos and comments from staff, parents, children and other visitors, with clearly defined next step action points.
- A digital screen showing evidence of daily practice within the rooms.
- Signs and labels in different languages and staff who are smiling and welcoming.
- Displays in the rooms that are not a clashing riot of colour and that truly reflect the children, with pre-prepared, computer generated labels and lots of photos of the children themselves and their activities, to reflect the routines and learning that take place. Such displays require thought and time, however it will be obvious that this is your consistent practice.
- Displays that also show captions from the staff, highlighting the specific learning that the other photos or children's work indicate.

Staff

The ultimate goal is to have staff who are clearly happy to be in the setting and who enjoy their jobs. Parents, visitors and Inspectors all want to see and feel a calm and organised atmosphere where the observed interaction between staff is professional and pleasant. Obvious indicators of staff's involvement with the children will be evident immediately by:

- What the staff are actually doing. In the best settings, practitioners are always, as far as possible, engaging with the children;
- They are using specific language to support and encourage and are clearly warm and nurturing in their approach;
- They are smiling and confident to talk to anyone who comes in to the room and to explain what they are doing and why;
- They are clearly well informed of the setting's procedures and systems and can demonstrate their individual input and opinions.

The paper evidence for all of this will be in the clearly displayed planning, the learning journals or other chosen means of recording individual children's progress and development. The manager, for his or her part, will be able to demonstrate all the necessary appraisal and monitoring forms, qualifications and certificates, policies, procedures and systems evidence.

I would strongly advise, however against the grain it may be, that you ensure all your paperwork is well organised; folders clearly labelled, easy to read and easy to access. There is nothing worse than going in to a setting where you can see the physical evidence of *outstanding* practice but then have to sift through chaotic paperwork in order see further evidence. Remember, the easier you can make it for someone to see what you do and why, the more quickly and clearly they will be able to make the most informed judgement.

3. Recruiting and Retaining the Best Staff

Alone, or with the other decision makers, you have identified your ideal by defining a *clearly outstanding* setting and this will have included the ideal number of staff with the right mix of personal qualities, experience and qualifications. It is all too easy at this point to feel overwhelmed by what your current reality is and the difficulties you have in managing your existing group of staff, particularly if there are members that you did not personally recruit but have inherited.

By looking at what you currently have in place, some issues that will have come up may include:

- Having enough money to fund the desired as opposed to minimum staff-to-children ratio;
- Having enough staff with the right level of qualifications;
- Having a good mix of staff that includes experienced leaders with enthusiastic apprentices;
- Staff with the right attitude, qualities and manner;
- The right systems in place to create the best working environment, clear expectations, fair and consistent performance management and a clear investment in Continuous Professional Development;

- A substantial 'bank account' of mutual trust and a give and take ethos.

This last point may have you frowning in confusion and wondering what it means and how it is relevant.

Very rarely, if ever, do people choose to work within Early Years for the financial reward. This is not, at present, a profession that is adequately financially rewarded considering the hours and level of responsibility placed on those who work in it. Practitioners in an Early Years setting, particularly those who are with the three to five years age group, have to fulfil exactly the same requirements as those expected of a qualified Reception Teacher but on a quarter of the pay.

There will always be some staff who do not share the same level of passion or commitment as others and it is therefore vital that you, as the owner or manager, are crystal clear, not only about your ethos and what you expect from your staff, but also about what your staff can expect from you. Employers in this sector have to work much harder to retain good staff members and make them feel sufficiently valued to continually do a good job, thus creating the right environment for the children in their care to learn and flourish.

Much emphasis is placed on the importance of developing children's independence, confidence, abilities and self-esteem. If this is not first fostered in the staff then how can they successfully and consistently create that in the children?

This chapter looks at how the above issues can be addressed and overcome. Case studies and tips will be offered as a means to gain clarity and help you decide what you wish to commit to in terms of establishing the right systems and lines of communication to achieve the best possible work atmosphere and practice.

Resources found at the end of this chapter are; useful questions to include in your interview process, strategies for identifying the qualities you want to develop and examples of questions and formats for how you appraise and develop your staff.

Let's look at the list of potential obstacles currently preventing you from having your ideal staff and working environment.

What is the right number of staff?

This is very much down to your individual interpretation and circumstances. Does it mean adhering to the EYFS legal guidelines of minimum adult to child ratio or does it mean always having extra staff members to ensure that there is time for effective planning, resource organisation and record keeping?

The EYFS sets out specific guidelines for this and advocates a minimum requirement, to which you are legally bound to adhere. Here is a quick reminder (although I know you could rattle this off in your sleep).

- Baby Room: At least one adult to three children aged under two, with one member being Level 3 or above and with two adults present at all times.

- Toddler Room: At least one adult to four children, with one staff member being Level 3 or above with at least two adults present at all times.

- Pre-School Room: At least one adult to eight children, with one staff member being Level 3 or above with at least two adults present at all times.

This is the minimum requirement and the EYFS guidelines specifically state that this reflects direct involvement with the children. Additional staff will be required to cover breaks, holidays, sickness etc. and may also be needed to undertake management tasks, maintain premises and equipment or tend to planning, resources and assessment.

While this is a minimum guideline, the EYFS document places the onus firmly with the provider in assessing the needs of their individual settings. The emphasis is that there is always adequate supervision of children and that the needs of those individual children being cared for are met. This also includes provision for sickness, maternity cover and general absenteeism which can create huge disruptions to the most organised of systems and plans.

We are back again, then, to creating clarity about what *outstanding* means specifically for you and your setting and how you prioritise to make it a reality.

The following case study illustrates the potential conflict these questions raise:

Case Study

I attended a meeting at a setting where the Finance Director and Nursery Manager were discussing staff ratios and changes in light of new funding and the departure of two room leaders. Other changes being considered were the steps to put in place to cover maternity leave for not one but three members of staff.

The meeting was a perfect example of different perspectives creating conflict. The Nursery Manager, knowing exactly how difficult each room is to run with only the minimum staff in place was arguing her case for increasing the ratio. The Finance Director was looking purely at the budget sheets and arguing that as long as the required ratio was being met then additional staffing cost was not only unnecessary but downright irresponsible to their business.

Things were further complicated by the manager trying to appease long standing staff members by fitting their required working hours around the needs of the role rather than fitting the person to the necessary hours required for that role.

This is a very common issue as most settings have practitioners who work a mixture of long and short days which can greatly impact upon the consistency of staffing within a room and the systems for communication and monitoring. Often, depending on budget and established priorities, a compromise has to be reached.

Creating the right balance

In the above case study, the two directors used the Disney Strategy to see things from the other's perspective and reach a workable compromise. This involved re-deploying existing staff, changing work hour patterns and creating a different mix of experienced and less experienced staff in each room, with a specific training and support plan added through the Development and Action Plans to ensure the changes were both workable and sustainable.

It is important to recognise that being extremely clear about what you actually want, is vital in helping you find viable solutions to any staff management issues.

A pitfall I frequently encounter is the temptation some managers have to rely very heavily on staff who have been at the setting a long time and have become an integral part of the running of the setting. This can be both a positive and a negative and both scenarios come with other potential difficulties.

Let's begin by looking at the positives. You may have extremely reliable, well qualified and motivated staff that consistently do their best and who you may possibly lean on in times of stress or change. These staff members work established hours and are relied upon for mentoring and training new staff. They are fantastic educators and positive and encouraging team workers. This can work wonders if such members of staff remain motivated, involved and valued.

The less positive result is that these members of staff may feel undervalued as they are always put in the position of coping with numerous changes in daily routines and systems that detract from their usual role and professional development. They may also feel resentful if they are asked to always be the one to carry less experienced staff or if they are not able to continue working the hours and times that have been previously agreed. They may also dislike change and disruption to their room routine if constantly inundated with new and inexperienced staff members who do not yet have the necessary knowledge, skills and capabilities to match their established model of *outstanding* practice.

I'm sure that this is a very familiar scenario for you and often can't be helped. This is where having a clear interpretation of *outstanding* becomes essential in creating and committing to the best possible practice and systems to uphold that interpretation.

To help you gain clarity and examine your existing practice, consider:

- How valued to do your staff members feel?
- How do you know?
- Can I always rely on them or is their resentment going to grow into negative and uncooperative behaviour?
- If Ofsted visit, will the staff in each room adequately evidence the quality you have asserted to be the case in your SEF?
- Do all the staff in your employ add value to the setting and to the children that are in their care?
- Are the children happy and thriving in the rooms where these staff are?

These are tough questions but a common scenario for where this may not be the case is when settings, due to budget restraints, continually employ staff at the minimum qualification level or an unqualified apprentice.

When Budget Restricts
Budgets and financial restrictions are by far the most common frustrations felt by managers when they are trying to create the best possible mix of staff for their setting. The intention to have the right staff, working

the right number of hours to suit the cover and systems you ideally want in place is always good but the reality can often make this difficult.

Employing less qualified staff may make sense financially but the impact on training, staff involvement, motivation and, potentially, the quality of care being provided to the children, can be very damaging. This can also make you vulnerable to the opinions of others who come in to the setting and make it difficult for you to justify and maintain your assertions of quality.

If we return to the argument between the Manager and the Finance Director, who was very strongly advocating the need to fit the person to the job as opposed to the job to the person, I realise how difficult this can be, particularly when you have long established patterns where staff members are working agreed set hours that previously suited you both.

It is not uncommon for many Room Leaders, for example, to not actually be the staff member who is there at the beginning and end of the day. Staff swaps to cover gaps in different rooms are also regular occurrences and, in some cases due to low staff and children levels at the beginning and end of the day, rooms are joined together to ensure the correct staff child ratio and attendance of the required Level 3 staff member.

This may work very well in some settings. Again, it comes back to being clear about what you are doing and why and the quality of the care and provision your systems create and maintain.

However, in my experience, such systems have created a wide range of problems that have led to a consistently disrupted and chaotic daily routine, resentful and de-motivated staff and a manager who is constantly rushing to the office to don a fireman's hat.

Such fire-fighting often results in the setting aside of those tasks you really want to be putting your time and efforts into, such as; self-reflection and forward planning, staff appraisals, monitoring systems, training and communicating with parents and outside agencies. Your time, instead, is taken up with; finding or being staff cover, contending with daily crises and conflicts, coping with continuous interruptions and distractions and managing increasingly unhappy staff.

I have painted a very negative picture here but sadly it is a reality that is all to present in many Nursery settings. This is particularly frustrating when the intention and care of the people who work there is good, but the clarity of systems and their purpose isn't made and kept clear, and the setting runs further away from, rather than toward, its intended *outstanding* status.

If your hands are tied financially and you have no choice but to work with your existing staffing arrangements then you, as chief decision maker or in co-operation with the others, must very clearly define what you feel the best staff mix to be, the hours that suit the individual needs of the room and setting as a whole and the personal qualities you need to have in your room leaders and the other practitioners.

When your current staff do not match your ideal

I have never come across a manager who is consciously trying to devalue and take for granted their staff, yet managers are frequently faced with practitioners who feel just that. This often results in individual members becoming increasingly un-cooperative and disruptive, leading other staff members to follow suit.

Frequently, managers inherit a setting that already has a number of long-serving staff. This may be fine but problems may occur if you are now managing people who were once your peers or are faced with staff who are openly distrustful and resentful of any change.

Being *clearly outstanding* may then appear nigh on impossible. However good the intention, if staff are feeling disgruntled, for whatever reason, then they are not going to perform at their best or represent your setting at its best and will lack the motivation and confidence to communicate the *outstanding* practice you are claiming to have.

For example, you may be experiencing staff who are openly resistant to change and deliberately make things as difficult as possible. They may demonstrate this through frequent lateness or absence, openly agreeing to all you do or say but bitterly complaining and moaning behind the scenes, or doing just enough to fulfil their job role but with an attitude of only doing just that, falling very short of enthusiasm, motivation and willingness to work as part of a team.

Case Study

A manager had worked very hard to establish the ideals she wanted to create for her setting and identified the areas that needed to be changed. Unfortunately, the setting had already undergone considerable disruption and change, including the threat of being closed down to lack of sustainability.

Having weathered this and secured external support from a range of sources, the manager was keen to enthuse staff with a new sense of purpose and with the other directors, held meetings to discuss current needs and circumstances and what changes everyone wanted to make, to secure a more sustainable and positive future.

Unfortunately, some staff had been in this situation before and had very little trust that any proposed changes would be followed through or sustained. While the intentions of the manager and directors were excellent and most of the staff were very willing, those staff who were sceptical were unfortunately proved right as the sheer enormity of creating and maintaining the identified changes and improvements became overwhelming, so the new systems that were promised were either not begun or didn't remain consistent.

The result was that some staff members became very disruptive, angry and bitter which had a very negative impact on everyone else. Though the manager did her best, she could not sustain any consistency in her approach and was forced to continually fire-fight new problems and issues that arose, leaving the complaints of these staff members to one side. A member of staff finally chose to leave under very unhappy circumstances.

This is an extreme example but it highlights the point that while there was fault on both sides, both were in fact behaving with positive intent, despite the negative outcomes.

All behaviour has a positive intent

It may not always seem like it but it is important to recognise that how someone is behaving does not always reflect what they are truly thinking or feeling. In the above case study it would be easy to assume that the manager was not doing her job properly or that the negative staff member was simply being troublesome and difficult.

The truth is that people's behaviour has a positive intent in that it may sometimes be a reflection of an unconscious belief or thought pattern, for example linked to low self-esteem or providing a secondary gain to them.

Think here for example of a staff member who never seems to be available for tidying-up time and allows others to pick up the slack. It could be that they are indeed lazy and happy to allow others to do their work (if they are daft enough to keep doing it) or it could also mean that they are unclear about what exactly is expected of them and when.

Before you shout me down, I have lost count of the times managers have said to me:

"But it's obvious what they should do, they should know by now!"

"We have routines that everyone knows about."

"It's all there in the job spec and staff handbook!"

"Isn't that what they teach them at college?"

There is no denying that in some cases settings have the best, most clearly laid-out and well-communicated job specifications, staff handbooks, policies and routines that are rigorously monitored, yet a staff member still doesn't make the necessary changes. But, as in the above case study, though the behaviour of the person in question is frequently negative, over the top and sometimes destructive, their complaints against the management always hold a grain of truth.

Discovering your options

With this in mind, work through the following questions and identify any areas and issues that are currently at odds with what you ideally want to achieve in your setting. Clear your mind of the staff and systems you currently have, this is about picturing your ideal, beginning with the end in mind and working out the best ways to get there. We will then look at some possible solutions.

- To meet your now clear vision of *outstanding*, how many staff do you ideally wish to have in each room?
- Taking in to account budget, ratios etc., what hours do you want them to be there? (For example, some nurseries operate a system where staff work from 8am until 6pm 4 days per week to ensure continuity for the children and to most effectively meet the requirements of the key person role)
- What hours, specifically do you want your Room Leaders to work?
- What balance of staff do you want to have in each room? For example, how many staff of which Level of qualification to meet the needs of that particular room.

- What, exactly, do you expect each staff member to know and do?
- How will you communicate these expectations?
- How will you make it absolutely clear about what is expected of them, why it is expected and the consequences if those expectations are not met?
- What monitoring system will you have in place and who will be responsible for it?
- How much time will you allow for room and staff meetings where reflection upon and review of practice can consistently occur?
- How often will you carry out staff appraisals?
- How will you train and support new staff?
- How will you manage staff performance?

I have deliberately put these questions in the future tense as the idea is to think about the ideal rather than get drawn in to reflecting upon any problems your current systems may indicate. I am sure that by now, however, you have identified several.

You will no doubt have clearly defined systems to all of the above but the point here is to raise the question of how effective they really are and how well they serve your clearly defined vision of *outstanding*.

Creating Consistency

The most common complaint I hear from staff in Nursery settings is that there is a lack of consistency and communication from the managers and that the systems, although in place, are not followed.

The reasons for this are varied but the result is always the same. Staff members often feel let down, devalued, taken for granted and resentful. The atmosphere and the environment can then become a breeding ground for negativity and systems are thrown in to complete chaos with an increase in staff absence or poor performance. Managers then feel frustrated as rather than doing what they want to do they are forced to fire-fight, contend with daily disruptions and deal with numerous complaints.

Having now identified what your ideal is, let us now look at the reality.

- What exactly do you have in place right now?
- How well does this match your identified goals and intended end result?
- How certain are you that all staff understand exactly what your vision is and their role in being part of it?
- In making any changes, what impact is there likely to be on your staff both positive and negative?
- If you have made previous changes that have not remained consistent, how can you convince staff that this time will be any different?

The need for trust

Early Years settings have, by far, the greatest number of external advisors and changes imposed upon them. It is very difficult to maintain the clarity and consistency necessary to make those enforced changes while also remaining true to your own beliefs, values and vision.

The same is true of your staff. To get the very best from the people who work for you, you first have to give of your very best to them. I have referred often to the term that "knowledge is power". If rules, requirements and expectations are made explicitly clear and they are managed and monitored with consistency, then people are happier to both receive and give some flexibility in behaviour in the spirit of creating and sustaining a common goal.

It is when things are unclear or are constantly changing that trust breaks down and the work place becomes a minefield for wrong assumptions, mis-communication and negative behaviour.

Trust is having the certainty that what you say will happen, does, and that every effort is made to value each individual's contribution to the work environment.

If regular deposits are made in to the emotional trust balance of the work place, there is far more likelihood that on the occasions where you do have to make changes, cause disruptions or ask for more than usually expected you will have staff who are willing to give more. Without exception, everyone wants to feel valued and that they are making a difference; they just have different ways of wanting those needs met.

Your job as manager is to be clear about what it is you want, what you are prepared to offer to obtain it and how you are going to maintain and develop your aspirations. Once you are clear about this it becomes much easier to recognise any discrepancies in individual staff members and determine if they are right for your setting. You will also then have clear, specific guidelines about how you deal with them; be it to nurture, train and support them or follow the necessary route to replace them.

Establishing ownership and responsibility

Whatever changes you may now have identified, it is vital that you are clear and consistent in the actions you take and in communicating where the respective ownership and responsibility lies, between you as manager and your staff.

At the end of this chapter, there is a list of questions to consider when placing an advert for new staff, example interview questions to determine a candidate's attitude and beliefs as well as their skills and capabilities and ideas for what to include in a staff induction pack.

In establishing your ideal staff ratio and capabilities, it is important to consider how you will be viewed by anyone considering coming to work with you. Before deciding on what you want from your ideal candidate, take a moment to consider and understand what they would like to know. Some examples are:

- I am looking at a job advert for your setting. Is it clear what the job is?
- What, exactly, is my role to be and what are my responsibilities?
- Is there an induction pack available?
- Does this pack tell me exactly what I need to know about my job, the nursery rules and expectations? Will someone go through it with me or do I just read and sign it?
- Will I have a mentor? How exactly will they work with me?
- Is there a review after a period of time?
- Will I be given specific tasks to complete as part of my training?
- Will I go on training courses?
- Am I given support in how to plan for and assess the children in my care?
- Am I included in room and staff meetings?
- How often do these meetings take place?
- Am I expected to attend these as part of my role or will I be paid additionally for my time?

- Does anyone monitor what I do? If so, how often and what happens as a result?
- Who do I go to if I'm not sure about anything?
- Can I approach the manager with any questions and do they take an active interest in my role and professional development?
- What communication systems are there in place?
- How often will I be given a staff appraisal?
- What will happen as a result of this?
- How do I put forward my own ideas?
- Will I be kept in the same room for which I have been employed?

There are countless other questions you may consider but the focus here is in being really transparent about what you offer and if working together is going to suit both parties. Once clear, ownership and responsibility is established and the expectations you express through your systems are far less likely to cause any future potential misunderstanding and mis-communication. It is then up to you as manager to remain committed to what you have said to establish the mutual trust needed for staff to commit to their part.

The same applies to your existing staff. Whatever the previous issues may have been, if you can show that you are clearly committed to the process of creating open and workable systems and lines of communication then existing staff members are far more likely to trust in the changes you are making and then display the behaviour, attitudes and capabilities that will create your ideal of *outstanding* practice.

The following are examples of questions staff members from a range of settings undergoing change asked the managers:

- Can I trust that when I come in every morning I will be in my usual room?
- Do I have to keep covering other staff?
- Can I trust that if I raise a concern it will be dealt with?
- Within what timeframe will it be dealt with and how will I know?
- Can I trust that when the manager says that something will be done, it will be – and if it isn't I'm told about it?
- Will I be responsible for mentoring new staff even when there is no allocated time to do so?
- Will there be regular meetings to discuss room issues and individual children?
- How often will this be and do I have to make extra time for them?
- Will there be enough staff so that the organising of resources, planning and paperwork can be done regularly?

- Can I trust that any nursery rules apply equally to all staff members?
- Will I have regular staff appraisals?
- What will happen as a result of them?
- Can I put forward my own ideas? If so, how?
- How will I know that they are being considered or used?
- Is there a consistent Continuous Professional Development plan?
- Can I be sure that my own interests and skills will be utilised and developed?
- Can I be sure that any additional staff member with whom I work has the right experience and qualifications to do what is expected?
- Will I be happy to go the extra mile for my manager because I feel valued and trusted enough to do so?
- Am I working in a thriving, busy and co-operative environment where disruptions are kept to a minimum and staff work well together because of their differences and not in spite of them?
- If an Ofsted Inspector or member of any other external agency walks in, will I feel confident to explain what I do and why and that I am fully involved with all aspects of the EYFS requirements?

Summary

This chapter has looked at how to identify and establish your own values and beliefs regarding the ideal number of staff and their ideal attitudes and behaviour, assess your current staffing levels and identify the additional resources you may need and the changes you need to make, common issues surrounding existing staff and the possible solutions to overcome them.

The next chapter explores the content of these first three chapters within the context of how you define what makes an *outstanding* manager and leader.

Chapter resources

Standing out from the crowd by creating the best job advert.

When placing an advert, it is tempting to rely on a previously used format or to rush it as you need to find someone in a hurry. This may well get the position filled quickly by a person with the right qualifications or experience but have you found the person with the right qualities and attitude?

If you want to attract the best person for the role you have identified then you need to make sure that you are making it easy for them to find you.

When placing an advert consider:

- Where are you placing it? Which publication or online vehicle?

- What size is your advert?
- How simple is it to spot and read amongst all the others? If you have too much text then your key messages will be lost. What is essential to keep in and what is relevant?
- What colours or typeface are you using?

If the aim of the advert is to encourage potential candidates to call for more information, what is it you want to say that will grab their attention? For example, a humorous statement indicating that those who dislike a challenge or require a simple life need not apply.

Don't be tempted to put every logo or information captions you have as a means to impress. What a parent or Ofsted Inspector is looking for is very different from what a potential candidate is looking for. Yes, it may be important that you are *outstanding*, but what is perhaps more important is putting across a flavour of who you are as a manager and setting.

Think of ways that your advert will stand out from the rest. Investigate where on the page it will be and what flexibility you have in choosing the best spot.

Additional questions to use at the interview stage to determine the attitudes and qualities of the candidate

It is of course essential that you are recruiting the person who has the best level of qualification and experience for the job. However, skills and capabilities can be provided through on-going support and training. What can't necessarily be taught, is the right attitude and personality traits that will give you a member of staff that is a match to your identified values and vision of *outstanding* practice.

There will of course be a mix of personalities and skills among your staff but if you have a clear vision in your head of what you are expecting and what you will offer in return, then any potential candidate can be assessed on how well they will fit in with not only your existing staff but your ideal in terms of their willingness to be part of your team.

We have already identified how you can make clear your setting's ethos, policies, systems and expected roles and responsibilities. The purpose here is to establish that clarity from the outset and provide evidence of your consistency. Perhaps you have used your advert to highlight key statements from existing staff on why they like working for you. However clear your expectations, staff also need to be clear about what they can expect from you and how working with you will be of mutual benefit.

With this in mind, the following questions may help in addition to your standard interview questions. They are not in any particular order but provide an example of what else you can ask to build a more rounded picture of your ideal candidate.

- How would your friends describe you?
- What do you do to recharge your batteries?
- In times of stress, do you prefer to be with others or spend time alone?
- What do you need to experience to feel secure in your job?
- What do you need to experience to have a sense of variety in your workplace?
- What gives you a sense of achievement?
- How do you like your achievements to be acknowledged by others?
- What do you do to challenge yourself?
- What makes you angry or frustrated?
- How do you cope with constructive criticism or with disagreements?
- How do you communicate your feelings when either upset or angry?
- Imagine your hundredth birthday party. Your partner, friend or a family member is about to give a toast to you and your life? What will they say about you?

This last question may seem a little odd but a person's responses will give a very good indicator about how they would like their life to be, what they are willing to do and how they would like to be perceived by others.

Depending on the age and level of experience of the candidate, some of these questions may not be appropriate or relevant. However, whether you choose to use these or questions of your own, the goal is to find out more about the aptitude, attitude and willingness of the person you are recruiting. You will then be far better placed to judge if they are the right fit for your setting and your clarity. Honesty about what you do (and do not) offer gives them the opportunity to decide the same.

Example Questions to use in Staff Appraisals

Most settings have a standard staff appraisal format. This may well be all you require but if your goal is to have staff that are happy and willing to reflect continuously on their own performance and that of the setting as a whole, then additional information can be very useful and valuable.

The purpose of an appraisal or performance review is to reflect on someone's performance against the criteria of an agreed job specification. In chapter eight, I have provided a model for giving and receiving effective feedback which could also be used as part of a staff performance review.

If the goal of a staff appraisal is for the individual practitioner to reflect upon their own practice and also their experience of the systems and support on offer by you as manager, then the following questions may be useful:

- Within your role, what have you most enjoyed doing?
- What do you consider your achievements to be?
- How would you like to build on that?
- What support would you need?
- Which aspects of your role do you find more challenging?
- What are the common obstacles and barriers you are experiencing?
- What have you done so far to address them?
- What other options are there?
- What new skills, talents or knowledge have you developed?
- What have you done with them?
- In what ways have you shared them?
- Have they been acknowledged? By whom?
- What would you like to do next to further develop them?
- What support do you need?
- What other positives have you noticed in your room or the setting as a whole?
- What areas can you identify for improvement?

- What options do you see for that?
- How do you see your role developing?

Using the GROW Coaching Model for dealing with day to day issues or conflict

The purpose of using this model is to not focus on the problem but to place the focus on finding the right solutions. This helps prevent sliding back into the habit of blaming, shaming and complaining and instead allows an issue to be looked at more objectively with a set structure for determining the best course of action.

By asking the right questions, the process empowers the other person to create their own solutions rather than be dictated to, which will create a more positive and sustainable outcome.

The following is an example where the process was used to help a room leader who was struggling to create consistency in the organisation and practice within the room. This covered room layout, planning and assessment procedures.

What is the Goal?

- What, ideally do you want the room to look like?
- What is on the walls?
- How would you like the resources organised and accessed?
- What are the staff doing?

- What are the children doing?
- What is the behaviour like?
- Who currently is responsible for the planning?
- What is the role and responsibility of each staff member?
- How is this communicated?
- How does the team work as a whole?
- What do parents say about the room?
- What do the children say?

What is the current Reality?

At this point, it is important to draw out exactly what the current situation is but in a very matter of fact way.

- What specifically is on the walls?
- What is the behaviour of the children like?
- How are the adults behaving?
- How clear is the current planning and assessment systems?
- How do you know that everyone knows what is expected of them?
- What has been provided so that the children are clear about room expectations, routines and systems?
- What is the current level of interaction between the staff and the children?
- What are the most obvious barriers and obstacles?

- Can you identify any gaps in knowledge, skills or capabilities?

What are the possible Options?

This is where you examine all possible options, even those that may seem totally unrealistic. The purpose is to think as broadly and creatively as possible. Again, emphasis should be placed on making the process as impartial and objective as possible. As far as possible, allow the other person to make all the suggestions and offer your own only at the end and with their permission. Examples in this case included:

- Establish clearer lines of communication;
- Have a whole setting meeting to determine behaviour expectations across all rooms;
- Establish how any changes in behaviour expectations can be communicated to the children, staff, parents and any visitors;
- Provide further support and training on tackling difficult conversations and delegation;
- Have visual resources in room to establish room routines and expectations.

What are you willing to do?

What is your will to commit? How much effort are you going to make? What are the markers for your success? Can you identify the necessary steps and effort required to move towards your identified goals?

4. So what kind of
leader are you?

To recognise and make any necessary changes to move your setting forward it is essential that you identify the characteristics of what you consider to be a good leader and then be really honest with yourself about how much you value those characteristics and which of them fits your own leadership style.

It is also important to establish here what kind of leader you are actually being allowed to be. This applies if you are the manager but not the owner and in situations where the setting is run by a board of directors of which you, as manager, are a part.

This is by no means easy, particularly as we are all prone to be rather blind at times to both our skills and our flaws. Our thoughts and behaviour as a result can be responsible for creating an environment that can be either *clearly outstanding* in its brilliance or *clearly outstanding* in its lack of it.

In chapter one, we explored the importance of establishing clarity about what *outstanding* means for all the relevant decision makers to arrive at a common understanding and practice for creating the systems necessary to achieve it. This process is often overlooked and the specific roles and responsibilities of each board member and in particular the manager, is not made specifically clear.

This can lead to misunderstanding and miscommunication about the manager's roles and responsibilities and therefore the actions taken in leading and managing the setting.

If this is the case then it is crucial that clarity and ownership at board level is first established. At the end of chapter 1 I have included a check list and helpful questions to discuss as a board to help this process. Once that is completed then the following process can be applied.

To manage a *clearly outstanding* setting you need to have absolute clarity about the qualities you have as a leader; the recognition of the areas in which you need to develop further knowledge and skills, the ability to model the successful behaviour of others; and the confidence to receive feedback about how others see you and use that information positively to move yourself and your setting forward.

This chapter will look at how to identify successful traits good leaders share, with specific exercises to develop your own knowledge, capabilities, skills and then identify any actions you need to take.

We will conclude with questions to assist you in determining exactly what it is you have to know and do to fulfil your legal and contractual obligations and how much flexibility you actually have in creating and running your understanding of a *clearly outstanding* setting.

What Makes a Good Leader?

The following exercise is excellent for identifying your own personal beliefs and then comparing them to the beliefs of others as the differences are often really enlightening.

This can be done either on your own or as a group exercise. Though be warned, when I did this exercise with a team of managers it nearly started World War Three, so strongly different were some of the views expressed. Remember the point here is not to focus on the person and their actions per se but the qualities they possessed as leaders.

On a large sheet of paper, write down all the people you can think of whom you regard to be or have been a good leader. They can be people you have worked with personally or from any walk of life, either past or present. Think about their qualities and why their leadership is or was considered to be so good.

A helpful tip here is that the purpose of a leader is to get people to follow them. How well do your choices of leaders do this?

Some examples of leaders that have been identified are: Ghandi, Jesus, Nelson Mandela, Alex Ferguson, my mother, Hitler, Margaret Thatcher, David

Beckham, The Spice Girls, Richard Branson, Winston Churchill, my current or previous boss.

Now you can understand how such heated debate came about!

The next stage of the exercise is to pull out the key words and phrases that best describe the essential qualities all these leaders shared and list them in order of how you perceive their importance and priority.

- Which qualities do you particularly admire?
- Which qualities have you personally experienced when being led by others?
- How effective are those qualities in terms of motivating people? For example, in the case of Hitler, while most people detest his actions, his ability to lead masses cannot be ignored, so how did he manage to do that?
- Which qualities do you recognise in yourself?
- Which qualities do you recognise that are not areas of strength for you? For example, listening skills, delegation, giving information, a tendency to make assumptions, well organised, inspirational.

Are there people you admire from whom you can learn and whose actions and behaviour you can model to improve your own leadership? This doesn't mean you have to physically meet them (which may actually prove very difficult if it is a leader you admire who is now dead) as you can learn a great deal from reading autobiographies or watching documentaries, which can provide a wealth of information about how that leader thought and behaved.

It can be argued that you can lead people and get them, as in the case of Hitler, to commit to actions and thoughts, through fear or lack of other choices, that are at odds with their values.

People will choose to follow a leader for a variety of reasons, both positive and negative. The following highlights some examples:

- Fear of the consequences if they don't follow;
- Lack of awareness of other choices;
- Laziness, it is sometimes easier to follow and complain than to complain and actually do something about it;
- Lack of confidence to do anything different;
- Lack of self-esteem, the leader must surely know more than me;
- Everyone else does;
- Fear of rocking the boat;
- Feeling genuinely inspired by the leader;
- Feeling valued and motivated by their leadership;
- Having an unshakeable belief in the leader's knowledge and skills;

I am sure you can think of many more. Debating the question of what makes a good leader could easily take up a book on its own and indeed there are many examples out there of publications that effectively do just that. The aim here is for you to gain clarity about what qualities you admire and why and then consider how well you fit that particular model.

Gaining feedback from others

In a busy environment where perhaps as a manger or owner you do not have anyone above you who can act as your line manager or sounding board, it is very easy to get lost in the day to day management role without having the benefit of reflecting on your own performance.

Staff appraisals and performance form the backbone of good practice in the recruitment and retention of suitable staff as we discussed in the last chapter. Yet very often, managers and owners are not afforded the same luxury to truly reflect on their own performance and identify evidence of their successes as well as the areas to develop and improve.

There are several options available, which will entirely depend on your individual circumstances but the following are options I have used or seen used in settings:

Peer-to-peer dialogue. This involves meeting with a trusted colleague or another manager in a similar role and asking reflective questions as part of a professional dialogue (I have included some sample questions for this purpose in the resource section);

Using your existing performance management format to reflect on your own practice either by yourself or, more helpfully, a trusted colleague;

Requesting a professional dialogue from an external agency, for example an advisor from your local authority or another professional you have dealt with and who you trust.

All of the above examples will certainly allow you to reflect on your practice, as will the Leadership and Management section of the Ofsted Self Evaluation Form. However, these will only be as helpful as the level of self-awareness you possess allows.

This is not intended as a criticism but we are all blind at times to our flaws and to how we come across to others. Finding an effective means to highlight our awareness requires a willingness to take ownership of our own thoughts and actions and what drives them.

Using Emotional Intelligence

You will have no doubt heard of the term, Emotional Intelligence. This is the term that indicates how well an individual demonstrates self-awareness and personal management. Indicators of how well we choose to communicate, how well we actually come across to others and how much self-control we show.

It can be argued that the most successful leaders are also the most self-aware but this does rather depend on the individual. Hitler may have considered himself very self-aware yet was absolutely single minded in the pursuit of his goals. In fact, research indicates that anyone who may have dared to criticise him or offer an alternative view point to his met with a very sticky end. I will leave you to draw your own conclusions from that.

In later chapters, we will explore more fully the skills and strategies that enable us to both give and receive effective feedback. However, as a manager and leader, it is essential to remain open to the views and opinions of others provided they are being given with positive intent. If they are not, and there are many circumstances where the aim of the feedback is to cause distress, it makes sense to have the confidence to be able to separate other people's opinions from how you value yourself as an individual.

There is an excellent phrase I was introduced to by a trainer who advocated that while confident people are always open to opportunities to develop and grow by listening to the views of others, they are also able to detach from the potential damage any feedback may cause by saying to themselves (or the person giving the feedback if feeling brave):

"Thank you for your feedback, I will consider it but I just wish to make clear that I am in no way attached to your good opinion of me."

This is a fabulous phrase that reminds us to separate the words from their intended impact.

Two specific feedback tools that work very well in gently showing someone areas to which they may be blind are the 360 Degree Feedback tool and the Johari Window. The purpose of both is to raise the receiver's awareness of their own views and opinions and those of others and therefore provides an opportunity for further growth and development.

The 360 Degree Feedback Tool

This is a very common tool used in a variety of business coaching and training contexts and is extremely useful for gathering feedback from a range of people.

The purpose behind it is to gain a broad range of opinions from all areas of the business you are leading. This means asking a wide cross section of people with whom the manager comes into contact, not just a close group, to positively or negatively view the person being reviewed.

The questions used are exactly the same for everyone and to get the most honest responses, the tool is best used by someone other than the manager. The feedback is then collated and presented to the manager in a report that highlights the strengths, weaknesses and areas for consideration and improvement.

The nature of the business and the purpose of the feedback will determine the type and number of questions used but below is an example of some of the questions I have used within settings as part of the manager's review:

- What do you feel the manager does well? Can you give me specific examples?
- What do you feel the manager does less well? Can you give me specific examples?
- What would you like to see being done differently? Please give specific examples?

Another powerful question to draw feedback specifically on how others view you is: What would you like the manager to keep doing, stop doing, begin doing?

The questions are deliberately open in order to elicit specific details without leading the person being asked. The purpose here is not to encourage a general gush or rant about the manager's qualities and flaws but to gain specific evidence of what, exactly, they are seen and felt to do.

Depending on the situation, you may choose to narrow down the focus to cover specific areas of management such as: Time management, delegation, communication and monitoring.

I have also seen an example where staff members were asked to provide specific evidence of examples when they felt inspired and motivated by the manager and examples when they didn't.

This type of feedback can be invaluable in allowing a manager to truly reflect on their performance and to identify any areas that need further development. This can be professional development such as further knowledge or training around specific aspects of child care development, finances, fundraising and grant applications, time management; or personal development linked to communication skills and the motivation of staff.

I must just put a word in here about motivation. A well respected colleague of mine, Liz, raised my awareness of the truth that, when managing staff, it is not a question of finding what specifically motivates people but being aware of what de-motivates them.

Of course, your aim is to create the best possible environment and circumstances that will allow you to develop the individual needs and skills of your staff but the evidence of when they are not happy or motivated is frequently easier to spot than when they are. Specific techniques for understanding the thoughts and feelings that lie behind the different behaviour and actions of your staff will be covered in later chapters.

The Johari Window

This is a specific tool that was developed by Joe Luft and Harry Ingram, two researchers at the University of California in the 1950s (Johari is the amalgamation of their first names). The purpose of it is to determine how far what others see and you see as the same. Below is a diagram of the Johari window Model:

The Johari Window Model

Open Area	Blind Area
Known by self and others	Unknown by self but seen by others Feedback required to develop awareness
Hidden Area	**Unknown Area**
Known by self but hidden from others Open to exposure through self-discovery and disclosure	Unknown by either self or others Can be revealed through others' observations of self-discovery

The ideal is to have the window pane in the top right, The Arena, as the largest as this is where people are most open and the views you and others share are mostly the same. The principle is that changing the size of one window will affect each of the others. For example, if you are as open as you can be and demonstrate self-awareness through your actions and communication, then you are far more likely to be considered an effective leader.

Often, managers have a large pane in the bottom left corner, The Façade. This is where you see managers adopting behaviour that would appear to make them confident leaders but they may well be masking insecurities.

For example, a manager who appears to handle dealing with external visitors very well but in reality suffers huge stress and nerves. Or the manager who seems to keep on top of the work load but only by doing so much at home away from the views of others for fear of being seen as inefficient.

In essence you spend your time defending what you believe are your secrets. This is both exhausting and can also mean your staff may feel that you are inauthentic as both a manager and person.

If the Blind Spot pane dominates then the repercussions can be very damaging. Your effect as a leader will be diminished as you may be perceived as just blundering your way through day to day with little awareness of your skills or weaknesses and without the capability to make any effective changes.

A large unknown pane may mean you are not only hard for others to read but your actions and feelings are also a mystery to yourself. You will therefore have very little control of what goes on around you or have the confidence to develop the clarity necessary to establish your setting goals and to evidence them sufficiently, to any of the people who have a vested interest in how the setting is run.

As the Arena pane is the most effective, there are two ways that you can enlarge it.

Ask people for feedback using some of the methods we have already identified.

Communicate more of your thoughts and feelings so people are more aware of why you do what you do.

With a trusted colleague, you can draw the window and discuss the chosen size of each pane and the reasons behind them. You can then determine which changes you would like to make.

Identifying the necessary changes

In using either of the two strategies outlined above, you will now be faced with identifying the specifics of what you do, why you do it and what you would prefer to do now. This is the What? Where? How? Who? When? Why? part of the process.

Of all of these questions it is the Why? that is the most emotive. It is far easier to work through the other questions as they can be used to deal with specific actions for development in areas such as the environment you create or the behaviour, capabilities and skills you possess and display. The Why? questions force you to consider where your beliefs, values, identity and purpose lie.

It takes a very rare manager indeed, to be truly lost in their blind spot and genuinely oblivious to the environment, opinions, actions and behaviour that surround them. Most managers have a gut feeling about what is working and what isn't and the following three steps can help bring you more clarity.

Step 1: Recognise that things are out of alignment

Your gut feeling is always your best guide for when things don't feel right and asking the right questions will help you identify exactly what you want to be different. For example, what changes do you need to make in your environment, behaviour, knowledge, skills and capabilities, methods of communication?

Knowledge frequently comes up as an area for development. Some managers may have completed their child care training some years ago and while they recognise the need to continually train and develop their staff, they frequently miss out on the opportunity to refresh their own knowledge or skills or keep updated with new initiatives that will help improve their practice.

Lack of knowledge or updated skills on the part of the manager will obviously then impact on the level of knowledge expected of the staff. Key questions to consider are:

- How confident are you that you possess the necessary knowledge about the essentials of child development?
- How confident are you that the practitioners you employ possess the right knowledge, capabilities and skills?
- What impact is this having on the quality of the education and care on offer and the attitudes and behaviour of the staff as part of the whole practice?

Step 2: Discover where the change really needs to take place

In so many cases I have seen managers struggle to make effective and long-term changes because they focus on the symptoms of an issue rather than the cause.

For example, staff members who are being disruptive or consistently not displaying the attitudes, initiative and skills you would like. Questions to consider are:

- How clear have I made my expectations and how consistent am I in monitoring them?
- What capabilities and skills do these practitioners actually possess and is there a knowledge gap I can fill by offering support or training?
- Do I possess the necessary knowledge, skills and capabilities to support them?
- Where can I go to get the necessary knowledge, skills and strategies to understand what I want them to do and how I expect them to do it?

Step 3: Once you have identified where the real change needs to take place, create the steps and actions needed to bring things back in to alignment

This is where all the tools and strategies in this book will help you. Unless you can gain clarity about your own feelings, beliefs, values and priorities, you won't be able to identify where in your setting these are not being matched.

To make any change there must be three things firmly in place for it to happen and be effective and long lasting:

- You must want to change;
- You know how to change;
- You get or create the opportunity to change.

This last point may be done through existing or new resources and from gathering information, knowledge and guidance, either from those around you or external sources.

The challenge faced by most settings is having the confidence and ability to sift through the wealth of knowledge, skills and resources available, not all of which will be welcome. That is why it is so necessary to identify exactly your vision of what you believe to be *clearly outstanding*, so you can have the confidence to explore your options and make decisions and choices for what best serves you and your setting.

Sifting through the options

Here are some simple guidelines to assist you in making those choices.

Understanding what you are legally or contractually obligated to do as opposed to what you are advised to do.

The principal guide for all Early Years Settings is the **Early Years Foundation Stage Framework**. This clearly sets out your legal requirements in terms of the service and care you provide. Some of what it contains is statutory while other aspects, such as staff ratios offer a guideline. For example, you have to have a minimum number of staff per child but you have a choice if you wish to go above it.

Ofsted requirements and recommendations.

These are very clear and very specific but the interpretation of them can often be subjective. If you receive any recommendations as part of your report then you are legally bound to carry them out. However the criteria against which they judge may vary so it is essential that you gather enough information about the most common interpretations of an *outstanding* practice.

Your contract with Local Authority or other partnership agencies such as Sure Start.

These will vary from county to county and will also affect your funding requirements and options. It is very easy to assume that you have to follow advice or guidance from external advisors in the mistaken belief that to not do so will affect your funding or grant applications. This may well be the case in some points so the important thing is to check and if in doubt obtain some independent advice from a Business Advisor. Most counties have such an advisor available to offer business support and will help you make sense of any contracts or forms you need to fill in.

Question, Question, Question!

Remember that knowledge is power and by asking the right questions you can gain all the information needed to identify and make the changes you feel necessary in your goal to create or sustain a *clearly outstanding* setting.

Make use of any external advisors or agencies; their job is to help you. The goal to be *outstanding* is the same; it is just the interpretation and methods that may differ.

Visit as many settings and managers that you can who have been awarded an *outstanding* status by Ofsted. What do they do, specifically, that Ofsted highlighted as *outstanding*? How could you use and adapt any of the methods and skills to suit your own setting?

Read through Ofsted reports and gather as much information as you can about how they view the individual settings as being *outstanding*. You can build a portfolio of comments and evidence highlighted that you can then use as part of your own assessment process.

Use the above information to update your SEF. The Self Evaluation Form is not statutory but it is a very useful tool for reflection and focus when used properly.

Summary

This chapter has given you practical exercises and tips to identify your understanding of what makes a good and effective leader and what you may need to do to improve your own knowledge, capabilities and skills.

The next chapter will look specifically at how you communicate and will help you define good and effective communication and its role in helping you become *clearly outstanding*.

Chapter Resources

An example format to hold a Professional Dialogue with a manager:

Using a series of prompts, (see below) we explored: thoughts and feelings about the nursery setting, his/her role as the manager, the strengths and areas for improvement he/she can identify and his/her vision for making things even better. These thoughts were then transferred to specific action points to be developed into a coherent plan at the setting.

* How do you see the Nursery?
* How do you see your role?
* What are your strengths?
* What are your areas that you feel need developing?
* Describe your ideal self:
* Describe how you feel others see you:
* What do you feel is currently working well:
* What would you like to improve upon?
* What are your current priorities?
* What actions are you going to take?

- How are you going to make them SMART? (Specific, Measurable, Achievable, Relevant, Time bound)

5. THE ART OF COMMUNICATION

THE NEXT FOUR CHAPTERS LOOK at how to develop your ability to create and maintain good rapport with everyone with whom you communicate. Developing your sensory awareness and recognising the traits and patterns in others will allow you to truly influence your desired outcomes in the most positive way, while also establishing a sense of value and worth for others.

The purpose here is to widen your choices in creating the best possible outcomes. By becoming a better communicator and creating the best environment that will foster the attitudes, behaviour, capabilities and skills you require, you will more easily fulfil your vision to be *clearly outstanding* in ways that will benefit all.

This chapter looks specifically at what communication is. We can't help but communicate, be it through, word, tone or body language. We will look at an NLP communication model, and introduce the concept of how our communication uses the processes of deletion, generalisation and extortion. Understanding these processes greatly impacts on how we communicate and how that is received and responded to by others. Common pitfalls we encounter when trying to successfully communicate with others will be put in a contextual example along with some of the strategies and tools that may help you to overcome them.

At the end of this chapter, you will find specific resources and games to use in helping you and your staff recognise the ease and the danger of making assumptions, how to develop your questioning skills and how well you give information.

Body and tone

However hard we may try not to, we cannot help but communicate. Whether you give voice to what you are thinking or feeling or not, your body language will often say if for you, and if you do speak, your tone of voice will say much more than your words.

Having had many an argument as a teenager with my mother, who would take issue with what she believed my raised eyebrow was saying to her when I hadn't uttered a word, I can certainly vouch for this.

Does the phrase "It's not what you said but how you said it," also ring a bell?

I am quite sure that in reading these words you are probably remembering many occasions in your setting where you have felt irritated or uncomfortable with how some of your staff members communicate with you. The staff meeting perhaps where a staff member doesn't say a word but makes his or her feelings extremely clear by their body language and facial expression. Or an appraisal where a staff member is smiling and appearing to listen attentively to what you are saying while their toes are tapping, their fingers are twiddling or their eyes are anywhere but looking at you.

The fact of the matter is that the words we speak only account for 7% of our communication. Our tone of voice makes up for 38% and our physiology or body language makes up 55%. Small wonder then that mis-communication and subsequent misunderstandings are the largest contributors to the obstacles many settings face to achieving their ideal goal of being *clearly outstanding*.

What is good communication?

According to NLP authors, Grinder and Bandler, the three set capabilities and skills that make up a great communicator are:

- Knowing what you want to get out of the communication;
- Being excellent at noticing the responses you are getting from others as you communicate;
- Having the behavioural flexibility to modify your behaviour till you get what you want.

The key thing to keep in mind with all three is the power of influencing with integrity. Any attempt to negatively influence someone through manipulation is the fastest way to create mistrust and misunderstanding and will potentially create long-term damage to the relationship.

Knowing what you want to get out of the communication

This sounds easy enough doesn't it? Surely you always know exactly what it is you want to say and what you want the other person or people to understand when you say it. And if they don't understand then it is their fault as they clearly didn't listen or have a bad attitude or are just being deliberately difficult as you really couldn't have made yourself clearer.

If the meaning of communication is the response it elicits then creating the right rapport is essential to create the most positive outcomes and win-win situations.

You know when you have a good rapport with someone; you feel comfortable with them, their body language matches yours and you feel like you are speaking the same language with a common understanding. Physically you will typically have good eye contact and some of your body language will mirror the other as will the pace, tone and actual language you each use to express yourselves. To describe that connection, you will probably use expressions such as:

- You only have to say something once and they get it;

- He/she didn't say anything but I know they understood;
- He/she always listens well;
- He/she understands me and what I am trying to achieve;
- I love working with that person, we think so alike, work in similar ways and have such a great deal of fun.

Equally, you will have lots of examples of people with whom you do not have good rapport. You may feel on edge whenever you speak to them, you may be suspicious of their tone of voice or body language, they may not look you in the eye when speaking, you always seem to misunderstand each other, one of you will always feel the other is being critical in some way, you may avoid having any contact where possible or even actively dislike them.

In both the above scenarios, can you identify people that you have either a positive or negative rapport with? Some examples could include:

- A fellow director or manager;
- Any staff member;
- An external advisor from your Local Authority;
- A member of the Area Special Needs team;
- An Early Years consultant;
- A financial advisor;

- Members of partnership agencies, e.g., Sure Start, Health, Social services;
- An Ofsted inspector.

In all of the above examples, the assumption is that you would want to have as much positive interaction with them as possible as it is clearly in the interest of both parties.

Common obstacles to creating good rapport

In chapter three, I introduced the concept that all behaviour has a positive intent, however destructive or negative that behaviour may appear to others. We tend to take so personally any criticism we come across, or take offence at what we believe to be the true meaning behind someone's words or actions, but this is only ever the result of our own perceptions and our interpretation of another's map of the world.

In communication, whatever our positive intent, we often perceive it as a failure if the message we intended to put across gets lost or misunderstood. We have all been in the situation of feeling like we're banging our head against a brick wall trying to get through to someone and often crying in despair saying things like:

"I just don't know how many more times or in how many more ways I can say the same thing!"

Whether we choose to blame ourselves or the person on the receiving end of that communication is another matter. The simple truth is, if you continue to do what you've always done, you'll continue to get what you've always got.

If someone is not getting the true meaning of our communication, it is up to us to change what we do and put the information across in a different way so that it will be heard and understood correctly.

Case study example

It's been a lovely, hot sunny day and you return to the nursery following a long and decidedly sticky meeting that has left you feeling exhausted and irritable. You left instructions to your room leaders that morning to get out all the outside resources from the shed and wash and sort them as an activity with the children. Your intent through this is to encourage staff to engage the children more in outside play. On your return, the staff and the children are nowhere to be seen in the outside area and there are no resources to be seen at all, let alone washed and being happily used by the children as you expected.

You storm into the Nursery, find all the children and staff in the dining room playing quietly and you explode. All the pent up frustration at your staff not having listened to your request, of always shirking their responsibilities, of being lazy and un-cooperative come pouring out to be met with outraged indignation by the staff. You retire to your office, steaming at how difficult is to get things done, drawing on your memory of when other things have been disregarded and you work up an internal dialogue of anger and recrimination at past situations that add more fuel to the fire of the existing one. Staff return to their rooms angry and resentful, building several similar internal pictures and dialogues that reflect other incidences where they feel you were unclear, hasty and unappreciative at their efforts.

Your deputy then comes into your office and informs you that the children, excited at the opportunity to play outside had requested having the paddling pools out and all the staff had joined together on the small playground to join the children in lots of splashing and water games. When it became too hot and the children needed a change of clothes and some rest, they had all come in to the dining room to cool down.

Your external behaviour of ranting at your staff provoked an internal state in the staff. They may experience feelings similar to your own of anger, resentment, hurt and frustration, responding by being defensive, un-communicative and un-cooperative. Remembering similar incidences when they felt unheard, they choose not to try to explain and chalk it up to yet another example of your poor management and why working for you is so difficult. Their external behaviour of sulking and withdrawing will then pull similar internal responses and interpretations from you and so the cycle continues.

An alternative scenario

Having discussed your requirements with your deputy and the room leader you leave for your meeting. On your return, when you notice the absence of the children and resources in the large outdoor area, you take a deep breath and rather than explode, seek out your staff to find out what is going on. From past experience, your room leaders become defensive in their explanation expecting to receive criticism. Recognising that to respond to this defensiveness will only elicit further withdrawal and un-cooperation from them, you praise their actions and join in a discussion with the children about what fun they had.

In this scenario, by changing your internal response and making a conscious effort to acknowledge your staff's initiative in responding to the children's interests and needs rather than blindly following instructions, you have gained control of the situation while also recognising that your original aim of having the children engage in outside play has been met.

By practicing the art of distancing yourself from your emotions when dealing with difficult situations, you are far more likely to achieve your intended outcomes.

The above example illustrates the importance of being really clear about what you are trying to communicate and then checking to see if what you have said has actually been understood and received in the way you intended.

Noticing the responses you are getting from others

We have all been guilty of talking in short hand and assuming that the other person is interpreting what we say in the way we do. This goes back to the rapport you have with the other person and how well you have communicated with them in the past.

With familiar people with whom we feel comfortable, it may be safe to make an assumption that they will correctly interpret what we say and do.

However, if you have new staff or practitioners or visitors with whom you do not share such good rapport, then the scope for mis-interpretation is wide.

This communication breakdown can often lead to the decline of the whole relationship. This is particularly the case when both parties become very rigid and un-cooperative in their behaviour and responses to each other, leaving little room for the flexibility that would allow for the issues to be dealt with more productively.

Typically, when communicating with people on this level you will find there is little eye contact from the person you are addressing, one or both of you will be displaying hostile and negative body language and the tone of voice will be conveying feelings of implied frustration, irritation or even dislike. In such cases, you can be certain that your wishes have not been correctly interpreted and the response you receive will not, therefore, be what you were hoping for. The end result is that both parties feel aggrieved, which leads to a dramatic decrease in the chance of a *win-win* outcome.

Seven plus two information bites

Another reason why our communication may fail in its intent is the amount of information we give at any one time. We recognise in our dealings with children the danger of overloading them with instructions and information. To do so can result in them becoming confused, forgetful of all that they need to do and then downhearted when they sense, or are told, that they haven't met your expectations.

The same applies to adults and it is really interesting to see how different people respond to varying amounts of information – and then what they do with it.

Research has been conducted by Professor George Miller into the amount of data people can hold in their short-term memory, the conclusion being that a person can hold seven pieces, plus or minus two. If they are really interested in a subject, they can manage up to nine pieces, if not it will be nearer to five. Try it and see for yourself:

You are a lover of films and are asked to name as many films as you can that feature a famous actor in thirty seconds. Sounds easy? I'm willing to pay good odds that you didn't manage more than nine.

Now think of a sport you have little or no interest in, for example football. Can you name as many football clubs as possible within the thirty seconds? Well done to you if you manage to even reach five, I couldn't when I tried.

Now think about all the pieces of information with which you are bombarded in your setting. There is a constant stream of visitors, each of them bringing new information, strategies or initiatives for you and your staff to take on board and then incorporate into your practice.

Your own staff meetings, memos, routines and other means of communication all add to the mix. It's little wonder that each individual, already viewing this information from their own unique perspective, will have very individual reactions to each situation.

Deletion, Distortion and Generalisation

The processes by which we each make internal representations of the external events we perceive through our senses, are influenced by our many different filters and experiences. Bearing in mind that on a daily basis our five senses are assaulted by approximately two billion pieces of information every second, it is no wonder we apply some serious filters to help us either absorb or screen out what we receive. If we didn't, we would all be in a white padded cell by now.

Three of the most common ways we filter information are through Deletion, Distortion and Generalisation.

Deletion

Deletion is when your mind shuts out something even though you are apparently paying attention to it. There are so many illustrations for this. Examples include:

- Staff who are only listening to some of what you say in a staff meeting and so miss hearing vital instructions or information about what is happening or what is expected of them;
- Staff who scrupulously tidy up the room but do not pick up the assorted coats, jumpers or odd shoes that litter the floor;

- Staff who argue black is white over what you have told them because they didn't hear the rest of the information;
- As manager, you attend a meeting and bring out all your necessary paperwork except the notes you made, instead taking out the setting's snack shopping list from your handbag.

Distortion

Distortion is when you misinterpret information that comes through your senses. Think of a time when you have been walking down the corridor, overhear your name and then hear peals of laughter. You would not be alone in jumping to the conclusion that your staff may be talking about you in a less than complimentary manner.

Or, you may be sitting alone in your office at night listening to the howling wind outside and think you hear someone knocking on the window. You turn and see a large shadow. As you begin to think you are facing a ghost, a burglar or, far worse, a late visit from an Ofsted Inspector, you breathe with relief when the caretaker comes into view brandishing a mop.

Generalisation

This is by far the most common way in which I have seen problems of mis-communication and misunderstanding raise their ugly heads. We make a generalisation when we approach a situation and view it with the conclusions we have formed from a similar past experience that we assume fit the current one.

Clearly there are positives to this or we would constantly have to be re-learning all the skills necessary to go about our day to day living. However, problems occur when we make generalisations about the people with whom we work, which in turn create problems in our understanding of and working relationship with them.

Case study

For example, a practitioner with whom I worked had previously worked in a situation where she had been bullied by a colleague. In her new position, when faced with another staff member who not only looked similar but had displayed similar behaviour she felt the old feelings of mistrust and fear.

Unsurprisingly, this led to this practitioner being very distant with her new colleague who, in turn, caused that colleague to make assumptions about her, branding her as being aloof and stand-offish. Both parties commented frequently and openly about these feelings to other staff members until it became a sizeable issue for the whole setting. Imagined slights and assumptions soon gave way to concrete examples of bad behaviour and the manager felt increasingly frustrated at being in the middle. Events began to worsen as other staff began to take sides which then created a very negative atmosphere across the whole setting. This began to then impact on the environment and quality of care being provided for the children.

You can imagine how this would have appeared to an external advisor or Inspector. Far from seeing the staff and setting at their best, they would have picked up immediately on the negative atmosphere and the lack of smooth systems and co-operation between the staff in their dealings with the children.

This matter was eventually resolved through having a mediated meeting between the two staff members and a frank discussion of what had caused the issue in the first place.

Recognising how we filter information

The above behaviour forms part of our Metaprograms, which are our most unconscious filters. We reveal our patterns of behaviour by the language we use and once you recognise your own, it is very easy to spot someone else's. Having said that, we all change our behaviour patterns according to the specific situation and environment we are in.

Case study

For example, a particularly unhappy staff member in one setting at which I worked was very clear in expressing her dissatisfaction with the management team and the environment. She could be heard frequently and loudly complaining to all who would listen about all the problems she saw and her own ideas for how to get things done better.

At a staff meeting however, she had very little to say. She may have continued to express her feelings through her body language and facial expressions but she refused to be drawn into saying anything specific about what she felt were important issues to be addressed; when invited to offer solutions, she had nothing to contribute.

In this instance, gaining clarity about what specifically made her unhappy and what actions would make a difference would be better tackled in a one-to-one conversation or in a staff appraisal. The manager at the time however, found this staff member very difficult to deal with. She used all manner of generalisations to describe the staff member's behaviour, what she perceived the problem to be and deleted any evidence that proved contrary to her set opinion. In essence both people were using their individual interpretation of the external events to validate their pre-existing opinions and the potential to resolve the issue became increasingly difficult as neither was willing to change tack.

We all see the same event or hear the same information with a slightly different perspective.

Think, for example, a staff meeting you may have recently held to deliver some new information or training. If you were to ask each staff member in turn what they heard and understood from that meeting, they would all say something slightly different. If the majority of your staff can tell you the main points and what they are now expected to do you obviously did your job well. If not, it may be time to reconsider what you are saying and how you are saying it.

To create positive rapport and become more effective in your communication, it is very useful to gain understanding of your own model before trying to determine another's. The aim of any communication is to effectively put across your intended meaning and get the response and outcome you require.

For this there is a lot of wisdom in the old sayings of: "Think before you speak" and "Count to ten before reacting to anything". Having greater understanding of how to positively influence communication with others can be tremendously liberating as it can give you the confidence to stay calm, focused on your outcome and more generous, kind and flexible in your dealings with others.

Summary

In this chapter we have explored what elements help us be effective communicators and the common reasons for so much mis-communication and misunderstanding in our working relationships.

The next step is to look closely at how you currently communicate and evaluate where you can make yourself more clear. For example, look back to the areas covered in chapter three:

- How do you communicate key information?
- Where do you feel that you may be making assumptions that everyone understands what you communicate?
- With whom do you have a good rapport and who do you need to make more effort with to understand their point of view and how well they receive the information you give?

In the next chapter we will look specifically at how you can develop more positive influence with people through the exploration of the Visual, Auditory and Kinaesthetic models and how these models influence our perceptions, language and behaviour, which can lead to more positive outcomes.

Chapter resources
Three Games
- **Snow Drift – making assumptions**
- **Who am I? – questioning game**
- **Taboo, Blind Dog – exercises for effective communication**

Snow Drift

This is a story that you read aloud to a group of people. Having done so, some statements associated with the story are read out and the listeners then decide if each statement is true or false.

This is a wonderful exercise to highlight how quickly we make assumptions and how often we make deletions, distortions and generalisations when receiving information.

When reading the story, keep your voice as neutral as possible and read at a normal story telling pace.

The story

Once upon a time, a beautiful cottage nestled in a shaded area of woodland near the kingdom of Frump. In the centre of the town, was a large bungalow, where lived a Queen with her pet dog. The Queen disliked walking and hated mirrors even more.

In the beautiful cottage, lived a young girl called Snow Drift. She was a gorgeous girl, who hid a great sadness, having been separated from her parents and banished to the woods where she was looked after by a group of snippets. She had mirrors everywhere and was popular with people and animals alike but had a reputation for being a bit unfocused. However, she was extremely good at healing.

The Queen hated her daughter. The dog, Prince Fur Face Paddy Paws, loved her and missed her very much.

One day, Prince Fur Face Paddy Paws became ill. The Queen was wheeled out on to her veranda where she addressed her subjects.

"Prince Fur Face is ill! I will give a handsome reward to anyone who can cure him and also find out who poisoned him."

News of this reward reached Snow Drift who at once felt sympathy at the plight of poor Prince Fur Face.

"I must go immediately!" she cried to the messenger.

"But , Snow Drift, you are not allowed to cross the big river in to Frump!"

"Never mind about that, I will find a way!"

Snow Drift immediately went to her friends, the snippets, who helped her gather all the herbs she needed. They also built her a small raft.

Once at the bungalow, Snow Drift was taken in to see the Queen. Prince Fur Face immediately got up from his bed and snuggled in to his beloved mistress.

"You!" The Queen hissed, "I thought I banished you!"

"Well, now I'm back. All I want is to heal Prince Fur Face,"

"Oh alright," grumbled the Queen, "That can be your reward for curing Prince Fur Face and finding out what has poisoned him."

Snow Drift looked at Prince Fur Face and gave him a small blade of grass to eat. Immediately, he skipped around the room happily.

"What was wrong with him?" the Queen cried.

"Nothing," replied Snow Drift, "he was poisoned by loneliness."

The Queen looked ashamed. "You're right, I have surrounded him with misery and this is the price. I can't bear to look at myself."

With that, she opened the door and called to her servants. In they came and Snow Drift was once more reunited with her parents.

As they turned to leave, an ugly young girl traipsed in to the room carrying a mirror, singing to herself, "Mirror, mirror all a quiver, I think I need a lift. I'll stamp and roar, break down the door if you don't rid me of that snow drift!"

"Where are my servants," she demanded? "You know I'll stamp and cry if I don't have them and Foxy!"

"Enough of your wickedness!" cried the Queen. "I have given in to you for far too long. It's time I banished you instead!"

With a howl, the girl dissolved into the floor and the Queen smiled as she saw Snow Drift, her parents and the red dog wander back to the river.

What to do

On a pre-prepared flip chart, have the following statements written. Provide pen and paper and as each of the statements is read aloud, ask the participants to respond by writing on their paper either "true" or "false".

When all of the statements have been read, ask everyone to swap papers and then reveal which statements were either true or false. How many did everyone get right? What were their reasons for deciding which statement was true or false?

The statements

- The town was called Frump.
- The kingdom was ruled by an ugly queen who had banned all mirrors.
- The Queen had a pet dog.
- The Queen hated her daughter.
- Prince Fur Face had been poisoned.
- Snow Drift lived alone.
- Snow Drift loved animals and was a healer.
- Snow Drift had been banned from crossing the river.
- Prince Fur Face was Snow Drift's dog.
- Snow Drift was the Queen's daughter.
- Snow Drift wanted to get Prince Fur Face back.
- The servants were Snow Drift's parents.

- The Queen's daughter was wicked.
- Snow Drift left with her parents and a red dog.

Who/what am I? A game to help with the asking of open questions to gather information.

This is a deceptively simple game and a very enlightening one to play in a group. So often, when we are asking questions to get information, we lean towards the use of closed questions. These are questions that leave little room for answers beyond a simple yes or no. For example: "Are you going to come in to work on time tomorrow?"

Sometimes that is all that is required. However, in the interest of finding out as much information as possible to improve communication and rapport, then the questions asked need to allow for more informative answers.

This game requires some post-it notes with the names of various people or things on them and is played in pairs. Each person takes it in turns to take a post-it with a name on and then respond to questions from their partner in order for them to work out who the person is.

The first stage of the game is to ask only closed questions and score how many questions it took before the right name is guessed.

The next stage is to ask only open questions that require more information to be provided and to keep score again of how many questions were needed before the correct guess is made.

Usually, there are fewer open questions needed to be asked than closed to get the required information.

Some example names of people and items to get you started:

Staff meeting, brown sugar, custard, David Beckham, SEF, planning, The Queen, Lady Gaga, Madonna, Linford Christie, David Cameron, Harrison Ford, snack time.

Taboo Game for improving how you give information

This is an excellent game for increasing our awareness of how often we make assumptions or use shorthand to communicate with others, particularly those with whom we have a good rapport. Think, for example, of situations where some people are aware of an "in joke". How would their means of communicating appear to someone not in on the joke?

In staff rooms or training sessions, we often make the assumption that others will automatically understand any use of jargon or that they will get the point exactly as you say it. However, we all receive and interpret information in different ways and the object of any communication is to be clearly understood and to feel heard by the other person.

This game is like the old board game Taboo. You take a word from a set of pre-prepared words and take it in turns to describe it without using the word itself, so others can guess what it is. To make it even harder, for some words you may also ban keywords associated with them.

For example, the word "dog" could be described as: a four legged animal, a pet, known as being man's best friend.

When under pressure it is amazing how difficult we can find this! A favourite example is when a colleague, who did this exercise with a business group, allocated the word "Golden Labrador" to one of the delegates. Choosing none of the above ways of explaining, he got stuck on simply repeating the words; "Blind dog! Blind Dog!" as he could only think of the working dog for the blind association for that word.

Rather than change tack, he repeated the same words but in an increasingly louder and more frustrated tone. This speaks volumes (if you'll pardon the pun) about our frustration when we feel that what we are trying to communicate is simply not being heard. The point this exercise illustrates is, rather than get angry, change what you are saying so that you will be more easily understood.

Some words to get you going are: Golden Labrador, snack time, planning, observations, Ofsted, Inspector, rota, lunch, children, parents, bamboo plant, panda, resources.

I'm sure you will have fun thinking of lots more.

6. Using Your Senses to Influence Positively

In the last chapter we looked at what is necessary to achieve the most positive and effective communication. Creating rapport with the person you communicate with is essential in achieving the most positive outcomes but the right environment and recognition of how you use your five senses can also have a tremendous impact.

In this chapter we will explore the recognition of your sensory awareness preferences and those of others. We will also identify how you can effectively increase your choices in the creation of positive outcomes by developing other styles of thinking and how you process information.

As educators, we work very hard at encouraging children to use and develop all of their senses in their learning and play, yet we often neglect to do the same for ourselves or the other adults with whom we work. We get stuck in a rut in the way we think and respond to the world around us, which can lead to us being less sensitive to the preferences of others and so limit our opportunities to engage with them more positively and effectively.

Returning to the points raised in the last chapter about how we often distort, generalise and delete most

151

of the information we receive, wouldn't it be great to use the same learning principles we apply to developing children and open up our understanding and choices as we engage in the world around us? Not to mention that it is also great fun!

We will be looking specifically at how we filter our experiences using our senses; how we use our sight, hearing, touch, smell and taste to describe how we experience the external world.

Understanding how we filter our reality through these senses gives us the knowledge and skills to recognise the responses of others, allowing us the opportunity to adapt our own behaviour to create the most positive outcome.

We will also look at the essential skills needed to create (and also when to break) rapport, using contextual examples of how this would be useful in your setting.

Visual, Auditory and Kinaesthetic

You have probably all heard of the term VAK, which stands for Visual, Auditory and Kinaesthetic. Many educational training courses highlight these three areas as specific learning styles of which you, as educators, need to be aware and use in your teaching.

The purpose of this is to understand and recognise the different learning preferences of the children we teach in order to provide the widest range of experiences possible and enable them to engage and learn effectively.

You may have been taken through several exercises to determine your own preferences with the results being loosely categorised as:

- **Visual**—the preference of using sight and pictures when making sense of experiences;
- **Auditory**—the preference of hearing sounds;
- **Kinaesthetic**—the response and preference to the touch or feel of things, the reliance on gut feeling and body awareness.

All of the above will be evident in how someone's thoughts and behaviour are most reflected in the language they use. This then gives insight about their individual preference, which then allows us the opportunity to tune-in and match those preferences to build more positive rapport.

Let's look at an example. When you are on a training course, what kind of presentation do you most feel engaged with? Do you respond most positively to:

- **The visual** presentation—how the room looks, what the trainer is wearing and how they are using their face and body language and the materials they use such as a power-point or bright displays?
- **The sounds you hear**—how the trainer sounds, their tone of voice, the quietness or loudness of the room, the music or other sounds they may use?

- **The feel of what you are experiencing**—how comfortable the chairs and tables are, the temperature of the room, how interactive any of the materials and displays are?
- **A mixture of all of the above**—we naturally use all of our senses when responding to different stimuli but there will usually be one that resonates more for us than the others.

Case study

I have worked with many settings in establishing a new room lay out following the identification of changes that needed to be made to raise the quality of care and provision for the children.

In one particular setting, the new room leader wanted to change everything around and create specific zones to reflect a balance of spaces for the children to access. When I asked her to describe how she wanted the room to be, the room leader immediately went into an enthusiastic description of the colours she wanted to have on the walls, the bright displays, and the specific colours and patterns she wanted for the fabrics.

The other staff members of the room were asked to contribute their ideas and one highlighted the need for a large carpet area to quiet the sound of the room as the children played, the sort of music she wanted to have played throughout the day and a specific sound station for the children to engage in audio stories and games.

Another member described the need for lots of soft cushions, different textured blankets and displays and the use of scented oils to create an inviting atmosphere.

The conversation became very heated, particularly when I pointed out the fact that small children in particular may not like zones and are happiest when they can move freely about the room moving and accessing resources at their will.

Ultimately, for the purpose of providing the broadest range of experiences for the children, elements of all three ideas were incorporated, which actually does reflect how most of us do blend all three of these preferences together despite having a preference for one mode over another.

Recognising your own preferences and those of others

The following quiz is a fun way for you to determine your preferred mode but please don't take it as scientific proof. This will simply give you an indicator and can be very enlightening when used with staff and colleagues.

For each of the following statements, circle the option that best describes you.

1. I make an important decision based on:
   - Following my gut reaction or feelings (K)
   - What sounds best to me (A)
   - What looks right to me (V)

2. When you attend an external training course, you feel it is most successful when:
   - The learning points are clearly evidenced in a manner easy to see and follow (V)
   - A sound argument is made, with which you agree (A)
   - You feel positive about the issues and they feel right to you (K)

3. People can always tell if I am in a good or bad mood by:
   - How I look (V)
   - What I choose to say about my thoughts and feelings (A)
   - My body language and tone of voice (K)

4. If I have an argument or conflict with someone, I am most influenced by:
   - The other person's use of words and tone of voice (A)
   - Their body language and facial expression (V)
   - How I perceive them to feel (K)

5. When exploring my environment, I am most aware of:
   - The sights around me in terms of colours and shapes (V)
   - The sounds and noise level around me (A)
   - The way things feel and the touch of different fabrics and textiles (K)

Look at your responses and determine which you have the highest number of: V, A or K. This will give you some idea of your individual preference.

For example, Mostly:

- **A—Auditory:** An auditory preference may mean that you are very sensitive to the sounds in your environment and how you manage them. You are very adept at tuning in to others through interpreting their tone of voice and are able to pick up very quickly on subtext. You probably enjoy listening to music, speaking and drama activities.
- **V—Visual:** A visual preference may mean that enjoy lots of visual images, you like your environment to be eye catching and well designed. You may have an eye for seeing things in the long-term and enjoy watching sports. You may be extremely good at noticing people's facial expressions and body language and are able to adapt your responses accordingly.

157

- **K—Kinaesthetic:** You very much follow your gut instinct and are sensitive to the feelings and moods of others. You may enjoy art and craft activities and respond well to a rich and textured environment.

Of course, these are all just indicators but I'm positive that you are already mentally flipping through your staff and deciding which preference they lean towards. Just beware of making generalisations. Rather like the fact that someone's behaviour is not their identity, neither is their VAK preference. Everyone is unique and responds in different ways but to raise our awareness adds to our capabilities and skills in building relationships with others.

One of the key ways to tune in to someone's VAK preference is to truly listen to the words they use. Looking for patterns in how someone communicates will give you clues about how they process information and therefore whether they will be more responsive to pictures, sounds or words.

In the last chapter I mentioned how the purpose of communication is the response it elicits and that sometimes it can feel that the person with whom you are trying to communicate speaks an entirely different language. Any conversation can turn into a very frustrating situation. Examples may include:

- Trying to find ways to motivate a young and disengaged member of staff;

- A parent who doesn't understand the value of play;
- A parent who doesn't understand the reasons for your invoicing system;
- A long serving staff member who is afraid of changes;
- A member of staff who has a very negative attitude;

In the next chapter, we will be looking specifically at tackling difficult conversations by understanding some of the reasons behind what makes them difficult and by exploring strategies to help overcome them. For now though, it is useful to understand that sometimes two people struggle to communicate because they speak with very different language styles.

For example, someone who is very visual may struggle to communicate with someone who has a very auditory preference, leading to much confusion and frustration if both sides feel that their point of view is not being really listened to and taken into account. To illustrate this more clearly, the following lists Visual, Auditory and Kinaesthetic words that people may use to indicate their VAK preference:

Visual

See, colour, focus, insight, perspective, vision, it appears that, it looks like, a glimpse of reality, look here, it seems obvious, show me, tunnel vision, bigger picture, looks right, I see what you mean.

Auditory

Argue, ask, deaf, discuss, loud, hear, sounds like, say, shout, tone of voice, yell, so you say, I heard it like, clear as a bell, word for word, we're on the same wavelength, music to my ears, that resonates with me, that strikes a chord.

Kinaesthetic

Cold, bounce ideas, exciting, have a grip, grasp, movement, pushy, moving through, that hit home, got a feel for it, pain in the neck.

I'm sure there are many more words you could add to each list but the purpose here is to highlight the different types of words and phrases each preference is more likely to use. The more you are aware of your own preference the more alert you will be to that of others and you can practice matching the words and phrases they would use to create a more positive rapport and more effective communication.

Using Your Eyes to improve how you communicate

As well as tuning in to the words people use to express themselves, being more aware of another's body language is invaluable in helping you communicate more effectively. People's eyes in particular can tell us many things that the people we are communicating with have no idea they are expressing.

Grinder and Bandler observed that people move their eyes in systematic directions depending on which representational system they are accessing, calling these **Eye Accessing Clues.**

Essentially, this means that when people move their eyes in response to specific questions, you can quite accurately tell if they are accessing pictures, sounds or feelings. This is an invaluable tool because it will give you more of a clue about their VAK preference and allow you to then choose the words you use more carefully in order communicate most effectively with them.

Imagine how fabulous it would be to ask your staff who ate the last biscuit or who didn't replace the last toilet roll and have a much better idea of the identity of the guilty culprit.

Remembering that all tools should be used with integrity and to create a *win-win* outcome, the following table will give you an idea of the most common accessing clues and how to recognise them.

Eye Patterns

VR	**Visually Remembered**
	Seeing images from memory, recalling things seen before. E.g., What colour is your front door?
VC	**Visual Constructed**
	Images of things that have never been seen before, things that are being imagined or made up

AR	**Auditory Remembered** Remembered sounds and voices heard before or things you have said to yourself before. E.g., can you remember the sound of your mother's voice?
AC	**Auditory Constructed** Making up sounds that you haven't heard before
K	**Kinaesthetic** Feelings, the sense of touch, accessing internal feelings
AID	**Auditory Internal Dialogue** Where our eyes tend to go when we are talking to ourselves, internal dialogue

The following picture illustrates the kind of processing most people do when they move their eyes in a particular direction. Be aware though that some people, most often those who are left-handed, will move their eyes in the opposite direction to the ways illustrated below.

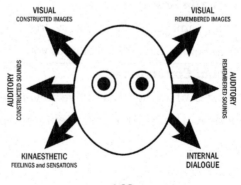

Developing sensory awareness is a very useful tool that will not only improve your communication in your personal and professional relationships but could also be an invaluable tool for understanding children's preferences too. This would be very useful in determining the type of environment and activity they would most enjoy and engage more productively with their learning.

Example contexts of where VAK can work most effectively for you

Influence a staff meeting or training session

In speaking to a large group of people you will be faced with a mix of VAK preferences. Following the use of the above game and exercise you could ask your staff to label themselves with their preference, e.g., give me the picture, tell me the words I need, let me know how you feel about this; but this may not be the most time effective idea! Instead, connect with everyone using a variety of media, such as a display or whiteboard of pictures and other visual clues, different sounds and tone of voice to engage the auditory and lots of references to feelings and sharing of your thoughts for the kinaesthetic.

Involving all your staff in redesigning their room

Encourage them to think about the needs of the different children in their care by focusing on the visual, sound and feel of the environment they are creating. Invite contributions about how bright and busy the room is while also having calm and quiet spaces, areas for sounds, use of music, the feel of the environment through the choice of textures and resources.

Establishing goals for the setting or personal goals in staff appraisals

Use the compelling future technique and invite the participant to imagine how the goal will look, feel and sound when it has been achieved. Imagine all the fine details that each sensation requires to be met and help them to move out of their preferred VAK to imagine other aspects to bring the goal alive and of their own making.

Increasing the power of your written communications

In creating job adverts and descriptions, advertising your setting, writing parent letters and newsletters and adding information to your website, think about broadening the type of words you use to cover all three VAK preferences. Really focus on the appearance of what you are writing, the visual, auditory and kinaesthetic words you use to appeal to the widest possible audience.

Connecting with people on the phone or in person

When talking to parents, external advisors, board directors or other outside parties, make a note of the kind of language they use (no, not that type of language though with some parents this may be very useful!) if on the phone so you can start to reflect back some of those phrases and words to help build more rapport. If talking in person, listen carefully and reflect back where possible, making a note afterwards of any words or phrases that stood out to help you in your next conversation with them.

Improving the quality of learning for the children

It is not the purpose of this book to suggest best practice but it stands to reason that by creating the best possible environment you are creating the best possible learning opportunities for the children in your care. A well planned and thought-out mix of visual, auditory and kinaesthetic resources and experiences is essential in providing children with the multi-sensory environment that will benefit their particular learning style.

More on How to Create and Break Effective Rapport

We have already explored how every person is unique with their own individual map of the world and way of processing and expressing their experiences through their thoughts, behaviour and actions.

In thinking about your staff members and other regular contacts, consider with whom you feel to have a strong and easy rapport. What is it about them that makes it easy for you to engage with them?

Similarly, think of someone with whom you feel you have little or no rapport and struggle to engage with effectively.

In both instances, what signals are you giving out through your use of words, body language and tone? What signals do you receive back? If you could apply what you do with the person with whom you have good rapport to the person with whom you don't, what would you do differently?

It is easy to assume that it is somehow the other person's fault and that they are difficult to get on with. Generalisation tends to come in to play here, particularly if you find other people who share your opinion of that person. Most people don't make the effort to change their own behaviour to create a different outcome, as it can take time and effort. But, using the NLP concept that the person with the most behavioural flexibility has the most power, it is worth making some changes in yourself to create more positive change and outcomes with the other person. The following case study illustrates this.

Case Study

I can remember very clearly the difficulty one manager was having with a particular member of her staff. The manager felt she never really knew where she stood with this person and found that the words she used said something very different from the tone of her voice and her body language. This goes back to that which we explored in chapter five; that communication is 7% words, 38% tone of voice and 55% facial expression and body language.

As other staff members had the same difficulty it was very easy to dismiss this staff member as being very difficult to work with and avoidance became preferable to communication.

The reality was that this staff member's body language set off an internal response in the people with whom she engaged, that caused them to feel uncomfortable and so go in to flight mode rather than confront the situation (More on this in chapter seven).

Ultimately, both sides built up a healthy resentment for the other resulting in the staff member leaving.

I am not saying for one moment that this particular staff member was without fault and was merely misunderstood; she did exhibit behaviour that had a very negative impact on the room in which she worked and on the children in her care. However, some of the misunderstanding could have been avoided if the manager had known how to alter her own responses and be more sympathetic to how that staff member was really feeling, or with that which she was intending to express.

Having good rapport with someone makes a huge difference in how they will view you and how tolerant they will be if you make any mistakes. Think again of how important it is to build mutual trust.

If you have invested the time and effort in building good rapport with people, they will be more forgiving of behaviour that seems out of character for you and more willing to make allowances, based on previous positive experiences.

Another setting with which I work does this by using every available opportunity to communicate with its staff and to make them all feel valued and appreciated. A whiteboard in the staff room not only keeps staff updated on daily news and important events but is also used as a means to celebrate individual achievements or examples of good practice. Even though the manager is not always there, she is effectively communicating to her staff that she has noticed what is happening in the setting and acknowledging the individual contributions they each make, as well as keeping them informed of every aspect of the day to day running.

This is incredibly useful in gaining the goodwill of parents, staff, partnership agencies and inspectors. How you present yourself and how open you are in your communication makes a real difference in the creation of positive outcomes.

Techniques for building Rapport

Think about the following examples and how you can apply them to your own behaviour:

The places and the people you spend time with

- How well do you make time for the people with whom you need to engage?
- Do you take time to create a calm and suitable environment in which to have quiet conversations or appraisals?
- Do you make time to engage with all staff members and not just those who always come in to your office?
- Do you make parents feel welcome and valued?

The way you look, sound and behave

- How aware are you of your tone of voice, facial expressions and body language when you are communicating?

- Do you make it clear that you are interested in what the other person is saying? Adopt a similar tone of voice and body stance to match the other person?

The skills you have learned

- How well are you using your skills to make yourself clear about what you want and expect from others to match your goals?

The values by which you live

- Do you keep your values and beliefs firmly in mind when you are preparing to communicate with others?
- Are you prioritising your goals and actions by responding, rather than simply reacting, to people or events?

Being yourself

- Are you being authentic in how you communicate?
- Is what you say and do a true reflection of what is really important to you?
- Are you hanging on to limiting beliefs that affect how you communicate? For example always saying yes to others to avoid conflict or confrontation?
- Are you able to say no? Do you end up fire-fighting because you can't bear to disappoint others or are

too unsure of your own beliefs and intentions to stand your ground?

- Do you automatically take on board everything an external advisor says and have negative rapport with them as a result? Saying "yes" but not meaning it is a sure-fire way to build resentment and create an atmosphere of mutual frustration and mis-communication.

- Do you have the confidence to listen to what others have to say but politely say that you will not be able to take on any further work load at this time as it is not part of an identified priority?

Knowing when you have genuine Rapport

In response to the above questions, you know when you have good rapport with someone when you both feel comfortable and at ease and are able to disagree without losing respect for one another or leading to mis-communication and confusion. The skill of being able to agree to differ is of great benefit, especially when there are choices in how to think or behave in a given circumstance.

For example, managers often find it difficult when external advisors push a particular method of assessment or practice at them and imply that this is the best possible way to achieve the best result. There will undoubtedly be a great deal of sense and merit in what they are saying or modelling but is their offering actually better than what you do already, or is it just different?

Knowing your own values and having confidence in your own beliefs and methods, means that you can listen with respect and not panic or say "yes" to things that don't sit well with you, providing you genuinely believe you can evidence the equal effectiveness of that which you already do (or are planning to do). Good rapport can be maintained by acknowledging the value of someone else's opinion and advice, while not having an emotional response that makes one or both parties feel devalued or that the other has been disrespectful.

The aim of having a *clearly outstanding* setting is to be actively evidencing the best possible practice. As you are working with a hugely broad range of people with various skills, knowledge and experience, it makes sense to create and maintain the best possible rapport with them to get the best value out of all the different opinions and views on offer.

You don't have to agree or take on board everything you hear or see but to remain open to it is demonstrating good sense and putting you in the most powerful position to create the best possible outcomes for your setting.

When you may need to break rapport

Part of establishing and maintaining positive rapport to achieve the best *win-win* outcomes, is to know when it is time to break it. For example:

- When you need a meeting or appraisal to end;
- When you feel enough has been said and there is no more to be gained by the conversation continuing;
- You need to give your attention to someone else;
- You're tired and you need to have a break to avoid the possibility of becoming emotional;
- You're genuinely busy and need to not be disturbed;
- The conversation is starting to move into uncomfortable territory, for example becoming personal about someone else or introducing a topic that is not relevant to the conversation.

How to break rapport without causing offence

Although we know it is the right thing to do, we often hesitate to break rapport for fear of causing offence and damaging the positive relationship and communication that has been established. However, breaking rapport doesn't have to be done overtly, subtle changes in your voice and body language will often be all that is required and still leave both parties with a good feeling of connection and positivity from the communication. For example:

- Changing how you look or physically move. Turning away, breaking eye contact, changing your facial expression, raising an eyebrow. Be aware of how you use these; remember how I suffered at having raised an eyebrow to my mother at the wrong time and in the wrong way.
- Changing your tone of voice. For example, suddenly upping the speed, tempo or volume after a quiet and serious chat. Staying silent will also create a powerful break but again, use this wisely.
- What you choose to say. I must get on, no thank you, goodbye for now. All of these will effectively indicate you need to move on and saying no thank you without any further explanation is a very good skill to practise.

Summary

In this chapter we have looked at some of the basic ways of creating positive rapport and also when to break it.

We have learned how to use the VAK system to recognise how you and others process and express experiences and how to recognise and use Eye Accessing Clues.

In the next chapter, we will explore more fully how to tackle difficult conversations using the knowledge and skills gained so far.

7. TACKLING DIFFICULT CONVERSATIONS

SO FAR WE HAVE EXAMINED the art of good communication and how to positively create rapport using our senses and environment. This chapter provides a practical guide to explain some of the reasons we find some conversations more difficult than others and tips and strategies to overcome those difficulties.

Specifically, we will look at:

- Feeling the fear, recognising limiting beliefs;
- The danger of collecting negative stamps and holding on to limiting beliefs;
- A brief introduction to Transactional Analysis;
- Practical ways to create the right rapport and when it is appropriate to break it; for example recognising and changing the *"fight-or-flight"* response" and dealing with strong emotions and negative behaviour;
- Brief outline of Giving and Receiving Effective feedback and what makes good delegation (which will be explored more fully in chapters eight and nine).

Feeling the fear

It would be lovely to feel positive and confident in all our communication with others but as we have already explored, that simply isn't possible. Life is constantly throwing us challenges and asking us to deal with situations and people that have a very different perspective from our own so it is only to be expected that, at times, we become fearful of dealing with them.

As we can't avoid those situations, especially as a manager, it would be useful to recognise the trigger points that create fear and apply some of the strategies and tools we have learned, to create more positive outcomes.

Below are examples of some of the most common reasons people use to avoid having difficult conversations:

- It feels safer to stay within the familiar, even if that means feeling bored and unfulfilled, rather than take a risk and really express how we feel for fear of rejection. For example, you find it hard to say "no" to demands placed on you by others, be it your staff, fellow Board members or external partners and agencies;

- The need to be liked overrides everything else. This is particularly common for managers who have been a long-standing colleague of the staff members they now have to manage. For example, having to provide feedback in an appraisal, saying "no" to requests for time off or having to tackle incidents where poor performance is becoming an issue that can no longer be ignored. It is a habit to constantly say yes to others and avoid making decisions that may make you unpopular, such as putting more pressure on yourself rather than delegating tasks, being firm about job roles and expectations and subsequent monitoring;

- Certain conversations and responses remind you of past situations where you felt uncomfortable and unconfident so you unconsciously shy away from them. For example, as we described in the previous chapter, someone's tone of voice, body language or use of language reminds you of someone else with whom you felt uncomfortable, which then dominates your responses (we will look at this more closely in the introduction to Transactional Analysis).

The danger of collecting negative experiences and holding on to limiting beliefs

First of all, we need to be aware that every time we avoid a challenging situation or difficult conversation we are actually storing lots of experiences that imprint in our mind and become a breeding ground for resentment, misery and anger. However hard we try to ignore it, at some point we will reach overload and explode.

I'm sure you can think of many instances where you have managed to hold it together for months then one day, someone pushes your buttons once too often and out roars the anger you feel at the current situation and all the pent up resentment, anger and misery you have been hoarding for months. The result is rarely good and the long-term damage to the relationship can be huge.

There are many reasons why we have the limiting beliefs in the first place and how they impact on our current behaviour. Here are just a few:

- We may have a long history of feeling terrible if someone is angry with us;
- We may believe that putting our own needs first makes us very selfish and therefore unlovable;
- Being popular and liked is preferable to being respected;
- It is terrible to let others down or disappoint them in any way;
- We have played the blame and shame game for too many years; it is far easier to blame someone or something else rather than take personal responsibility.

If any of the above resonates with you then you are by no means alone. We have explored many of the concepts of NLP to help us understand why we think what we do and how that translates through our external behaviour. As a way of explaining a little more about the internal and external responses that makes up how we communicate, I would like to introduce you to the world of **Transactional Analysis.**

Transactional Analysis

This always creates the most "A-ha!" moments in any training I carry out with managers. Once you have a basic understanding of its principles, it is absolutely fascinating to then examine why we have certain patterns of behaviour and how that then translates to how well we communicate with others. I cannot possibly explain all the theory and practice here but you will find an excellent book list at the end that will fill in any of the gaps and satisfy your further curiosity if it grips you as much as it has other managers to whom I've introduced it.

For now, let me give you a brief overview of how it can help you recognise any limiting beliefs you may be holding-on to and how you can overcome them.

Transactional Analysis was seen by the Psychologist, Eric Berne as both a theory of personality and social interaction and a method of therapy. In essence it is based on the following basic philosophical assumptions:

• People are ok.

- Everyone has the capacity to think so everyone can decide for themselves what they want from life.
- People decide and create their own destiny.
- All decisions can be changed.

TA can provide the means to become aware of previous decisions, which have defined how we think, feel and behave and see if they still serve us, making new decisions as we see fit.

These assumptions lead on to the main concepts that determine how we think and behave. We essentially have three **Ego States; parent, adult and child.** When we are in our parent state we alternate between being a nurturing or a critical parent. In essence, we are mimicking behaviour that our own parents displayed.

Parent state

For example, think of a staff member who drives you to distraction because they are always late, never seem to be on task and rarely do what is expected. With this person, depending on how they behave and the feelings they create in you, you may respond by nurturing them as would a caring mother or father. Perhaps they remind you of a younger sibling, favourite cousin or even your own child. You may complain but you will shake your head, say things like;

"Oh well, she can't help it, bless her," and then happily pick up the pieces and be endlessly tolerant and sympathetic.

The downside to this is that this person may never take on any responsibility for governing their own actions and other staff, who do not feel in the least bit nurturing towards them, may become very angry and resentful, accusing you of having different rules for different people.

Now think of another member of staff who displays similar behaviour that you do not warm to so well. You may well find that instead of the nurturing parent, out comes the critical. You will be very stern with them, intolerant and expect them to display much more responsibility for their behaviour. You may also complain about them and gather even more negative internal experiences by collecting similar opinions about their failings from others.

Either way you are not considering this person as a responsible adult but as a child for whom you feel responsible and treat accordingly.

We do this unconsciously all the time. For example, do you find yourself always trying to rescue people and fix them? Or do you find that you can be quite judgmental and intolerant when others display behaviour you don't like?

Being in this state can create a great deal of difficulty in how you communicate with others. The people you are trying to help and support may not always appreciate it or, eventually, you become resentful of having to always chivvy them along and make allowances, leading you to swing between nurturing and critical parent. Ultimately, this can create a great deal of confusion as well as an imbalance in the relationship, that makes dealing with that person in a professional way more difficult.

Child state

This state is made up of responses in which we think, feel and behave in a similar way to when we were a child. In different contexts, you may see someone being very adaptive to the needs and expectations of others, searching for approval and being compliant in many situations. Alternatively, the rebellious child will come out, wanting to go against the system, going off at a tangent and responding to criticism by being sulky and difficult.

When faced with someone who is being adaptive and gives the impression of low self-esteem, you may respond as either a nurturing or critical parent by either rushing to support and fix them or by feeling critical and judging as outlined above.

Adult state

The ideal state to be in is that of the adult. In this state, you are not being drawn in to reacting to someone else's behaviour but emotionally detaching yourself to treat them as an equal, ok and capable adult.

We constantly swing between all three states depending on our individual experiences, memories, thoughts and feelings and will certainly behave differently with one person than we do with another. These responses obviously impact on our ability to build rapport and gain positive outcomes from our communication but the trick is to be able to recognise the state we are in ourselves and adapt it to gain more positive control of the situation.

Essentially, this means managing our transactions with others and the strokes we receive. I do not mean literal strokes but the responses and feelings we have when we interact with someone that will either be positive or negative.

Like the children we care for, we will look for positive recognition and ways to feel valued and will display a whole range of behaviour to get it.

For example, if I asked you to think of some of the behaviour a child will display when he is looking for attention you will see such things as:

- Talking loudly and over others;
- Behaving in negative ways to grab your attention;
- Slamming doors and sulking;
- Withdrawing and refusing to engage;
- Becoming over demonstrative;

- Following you around;
- Constantly telling you how good they are;
- Puffing up when praised;
- Agreeing with everything you say to gain approval;
- Persisting with negative behaviour;

Does this also remind you of any adults you know and with whom you work?

Sometimes two parties with whom we are communicating are in the same state. For example, you may have two staff members that you try to avoid sitting next to each other as they become very childish and disruptive. This can be very frustrating and lead you to interact with them either as a critical parent where you try to control their behaviour or as a nurturing parent where you smile and acknowledge their antics but don't actually do anything about it. The latter will invariably lead other staff members to feel angry and respond either as a critical parent themselves or vie for your attention by acting themselves as stroppy, rebellious children. Rarely have I seen many of these interactions take place on the adult to adult state which would be the most positive way forward. A typical staff meeting scenario may illustrate this more clearly as follows:

Example

You are leading a staff meeting and have many things you need to discuss relating to some new systems and procedures you would like to introduce. As you look around the room, you can see some staff looking expectantly at you with relaxed and open expressions, some refusing to look at you at all and expressing their lack of interest by looking at the floor or out of the window and others who are engaged in a private conversation as you try to talk and whose whispers get increasingly louder and their behaviour more childish and silly.

You may choose to respond in a variety of ways and get the following responses:

- **You** (Critical parent to child): I have already asked you to be quiet and listen to me as what I am saying is important and you all need to take it on board.
- **Staff** (rebellious child to critical parent): I am listening! You're always picking on me. You're not saying this to Susan in the corner who's been talking and playing with blu-tac! Susan and the staff member you have just addressed may now actually join forces by giggling at each other and finding the whole thing hilarious, interacting in child to child state, in unison, against you as critical parent.

This conversation may well continue for a few minutes, playing games to create the most dominance but which is probably leaving you feeling that you would like to send the culprits off to their room without any supper.

Meanwhile, you try to re-engage with the staff that have so far been listening patiently to you and are beginning to express their critical parent state by frowning or directing comments to the disruptive staff. Others may be switching off altogether while others may now feel disgruntled at being ignored and begin to display some rebellious child-like behaviour of their own.

- **You** (Critical parent): I'm sorry that this is taking so long and that a few staff members appear to be spoiling what should be a very productive meeting. I have said time and time again how important it is to listen and for us all to be involved with what is being said, so that we can think like a team. Now I can't think properly at all and am feeling as frustrated as you, that yet again we are going round in circles and not getting things done!

The resulting behaviour may then include

- The original child-like staff continuing to behave in a foolish and disruptive manner;
- Other staff lose interest all together and stop listening;

- Some staff start talking loudly to drown out the child-like staff and talk over both them and you;
- You start to address only the staff you feel are listening and try to ignore the others.

What is frequently missing is the adult to adult interaction which is the most difficult to obtain when others are displaying evidence of a completely different state to your own. The only option then is to take a step back, recognise what states you are witnessing and be aware of the responses they are creating in you. It is very easy to simply react and get involved in familiar patterns of communication that don't serve you or your intended outcomes.

In the last chapter we explored how the meaning of any communication is the response it elicits. To bring about changes in others and have the confidence to tackle difficult conversations it is essential to keep the end result in mind and then work out the potential obstacles to be overcome to enable you to find the right solutions and create the desired outcomes.

Ways to create the right rapport and when to break it

The above example indicated how being led by the responses of others can create a spiral of reactions that quickly leads us away from our intended outcomes. Trying to avoid such situations and the necessary conversations that can be difficult to tackle is often the biggest cause of the mis-communication, misunderstanding and poor working atmosphere that hinders your desire to be *outstanding*. How can you effectively communicate and engage with children and other agencies if communication within your setting is not clear, authentic and part of your whole ethos in creating an *outstanding* environment?

Like the staff meeting above, there are some conversations where you will expect to receive resistance from others, be it from staff, parents or outside agencies. These could include performance reviews, addressing aspects of behaviour you are unhappy with, persuading someone to take on extra responsibility, asking a parent to pay their fees or dealing with an external advisor with whom you are anticipating conflict.

Tips to help you

- Have a clear objective of what you want to achieve and why;
- Be clear about the kind of response you want, what kind of agreement are you looking for and the *win-win*;
- Check how full the emotional bank account is with this particular person. Is there a healthy balance of mutual respect and trust present that will allow

you to ask for changes or say no to them without causing personal distress?

- Be aware of your tone of voice and how you look and behave. How you present yourself will make a tremendous difference to how you will be perceived. In the example above, for instance, behaving and sounding like a critical parent will not bring about the most productive response. Be aware of your own behaviour and expectation to engage as an adult, raising the same expectation in the other person
- Never give negative feedback publicly;
- Be aware that by offering any form of negative criticism you are potentially creating a *fight-or-flight* response in the other person.

Fight-or-flight

Receiving any form of negative feedback is never easy and will trigger certain emotions in all of us. Our childhood experiences and memories of how we interacted with key people and influencers will have a great deal of effect on our current responses. The feelings that different people evoke in us dictate our reaction.

For example, how often do we avoid talking to someone because their manner and behaviour reminds us of an old aunt who was mean to us or a previous boss by whom we felt intimidated? Equally, we may be exceptionally tolerant of a person's behaviour that we would absolutely not tolerate in any one else, because they remind us of a favourite cousin or grandparent or former colleague, lover or friend.

In chapter eight, we will look at a specific model for separating the behaviour from the person but it is important to recognise why we feel the *fight-or-flight* response and what triggers it.

Features of *fight-or-flight* can be triggered when we feel in danger. This does not mean just physical danger but when we feel our inner self is being attacked, for example if we feel embarrassed or humiliated and we feel the attack is unjustified or if what is being said makes us doubt ourselves as we feel it may contain some truth but we don't like to acknowledge it. These responses can generally be characterised by:

Flight
- Avoidance of eye contact,
- Withdrawal and not saying much,
- Fidgeting,
- Speaking quietly or stuttering,
- Flushing,
- Adopting a submissive pose – head down, shoulders hunched.

Fight
- Strong eye contact,

- Talking more loudly,
- Moving closer to the other person,
- Jabbing gestures,
- More animation in voice or hand movements,
- Speaking over the other person.

Ways to control *fight-or-flight* responses

The first step is to notice how you are feeling and prevent those feelings from taking you over, remaining, as far as possible in the productive adult state. It is impossible not to have an emotional reaction to external events but it is possible to acknowledge your feelings without having to display them. By deliberately creating the right circumstances for the conversation beforehand and taking time to listen and understand what others are saying before responding, will make a great difference to you achieving your intended outcome.

Summary

This chapter has provided you with some practical situations in which to recognise why we find some conversations difficult. It has also given some practical solutions to change our own behaviour and so influence more positively, the behaviour of others.

In the next chapter we will look in more detail at how to control positively, our own responses and those of others, to create a *win-win* outcome, along with a practical format for how to give and receive feedback in a range of situations.

8. Strategies for Giving and Receiving Feedback

IN THE LAST CHAPTER, WE looked at what can make certain conversations difficult and how to recognise the responses in ourselves and others so that we can change those difficulties into the creation of more positive outcomes.

In this chapter we will look at how we can more effectively create the right environment and circumstances to enable more positive communication. We will also look in detail at the **BOCA** (Behaviour, Outcomes, Consequences and Actions) model for giving and receiving effective feedback, using a range of contextual examples.

There are resources at the end of this chapter to illustrate how the **BOCA** model can be used most effectively.

Examples of difficult conversations

There are lots of situations in which we shy away from having difficult conversations and we have already looked at some of them. However, as a manager, the way you communicate will set the tone for how the whole setting communicates and any changes that you feel need to be made start with you first and then work down. In the courses I lead for Early Years settings, the most common areas of difficulty include:

- Managing staff meetings;
- Performance reviews;
- Dealing with consistent incidences of poor behaviour;
- Dealing with difficult parents;
- Handling conflict between staff members;
- Talking to outside agencies or Ofsted Inspectors.

In all of the above situations you may either be the giver or the receiver of criticism, neither of which is pleasant to deal with. We have looked at the *fight-or-flight* response that such situations create and some ways to overcome those responses but there are other techniques that can help you raise awareness of your own behavioural responses and be more sensitive to those of others.

The purpose, as always, is to keep the end firmly in mind and create the most positive outcomes by managing your own behaviour to more effectively influence the behaviour of others.

We looked at an example in the previous chapter of some of the difficulties in managing staff meetings and groups of people as well as individuals. Whether it is one-to-one or a group situation, creating the right environment can be crucial to the success of the intended interaction.

Going back to how to use your senses to create the right environment and circumstances for building rapport, helpful tips include:

Creating the right environment

This will very much depend on the size and layout of your particular setting and I am very aware that some settings don't have the luxury of a training room or small office where such meetings can most effectively take place. Often, in these cases, meetings have to take place in the actual rooms the children occupy or in small offices that are multi-purpose in their use.

If this is the case then forward planning is essential. There will occasionally be instances where something has be dealt with immediately, in which case you have to go with what you've got and make best use of some of the other strategies we will look at, to create the right atmosphere and sense of rapport.

Often though, you can plan a meeting with a parent or staff member which will allow you the time to adequately prepare both the environment and your own feelings.

If you do have a separate space you can use think carefully about the atmosphere and environment you want to create:

- Is the room private and can you ensure you won't be interrupted?
- Is it tidy and free from clutter?

- Is it welcoming?
- Do you have comfortable chairs and furnishings?
- Do you have the necessary resources to hand, i.e., water, tissues, writing utensils, relevant paperwork etc.?

Managing Expectations

This leads us back to section one where you established very clearly what you want to communicate to your staff, parents and other external parties and your methods for doing so.

This is an extension of that, where you now make very clear your own expectations for the outcome of the communication and how you will consider the impact on others beforehand.

Much of this will be laid out in your handbooks and policies but you may want to create a separate guideline to explain your expectations in staff meetings, staff appraisals and any procedures for managing complaints. You will also want to consider the lines of communication in your setting and how clearly they are laid out and managed.

There is a danger, particularly when dealing with the range of requests and demands placed on you by staff, parents and other partners, of raising expectations to such a level that you consistently over promise and under deliver.

For example, you may tell parents that of course they can have complete flexibility on their payment structure or times for dropping and picking up, only to then have to change that promise when it negatively impacts on the setting in some way.

Similarly, you may consistently promise staff you will find time to have staff appraisals or meetings that you fail to make happen because other things get in the way. You may promise to delegate more or deal with how the planning and rotas in a particular way are not working but fail to do so.

The key is to create the right systems that will work for your setting and then communicate them clearly through both what you say and what you do. If people know what to expect they will be less likely to become frustrated when things go wrong and will have trust that you will do your best to manage the situation.

Useful phrases to say to parents

- I understand that you are upset about this. Let me show you our policy and the agreement you signed and we can see how we can best move forward.
- I am sorry you feel that way, please tell me what specifically you are unhappy about and the outcome you would like so we can agree on how to best move forward.

- I won't be able to meet that requirement as it doesn't comply with our policy. Can we discuss how else we may be able to meet your needs?

Useful phrases to say to staff

- I can't accommodate your request at the moment. Can we discuss an alternative that suits both you and the needs of the setting?
- I won't be able to complete the staff appraisals this month. If time becomes available I will let you know but let's block some time in the diary for a mutually convenient date next month.
- I appreciate that you do not like the new working hours but these are the times that suit the role and needs of the children. I cannot promise to accommodate your needs but am prepared to look at alternatives that will suit us both.
- We have two hours for this staff meeting and I expect to get through these items on the agenda. I appreciate this may not give enough time to allow you all to express your views on each point but we will highlight those that require further discussion and find another time to address them.

Useful phrases to say to partners or outside agencies

- I won't be able to meet that deadline. Can we discuss extending it?

- I appreciate that this is a priority for you. However, our current priorities lie here. Can we discuss how we can agree on which aspects we will both consider and plan for when to address the other items at a later date?

- I agree that your suggestions are important and I will discuss this with my team at our next staff meeting. However, I cannot promise that we will reach a decision until after the holiday or until we have addressed the other priority items on our plan.

In all of the above examples, there will inevitably be situations where strong feelings will be running high, which may well jeopardise the intended positive outcome. The feelings may be yours when you are experiencing feelings of frustration, anger or being overwhelmed by all you have to do or with which you have to cope.

Others may express anger, resentment, fear, upset or outrage depending upon a range of situations and contexts. Recognising when such feelings are occurring and having the ability to diffuse them, will help you overcome any barriers to tackling difficult conversations that may arise as a result.

Expressing strong feelings and how to manage them

However hard you may try or whatever expectations you have laid down, there will inevitably be occurrences where feelings will run high or you or a staff member may bring those feelings into the work place. The regularity with which this happens will determine the course of action you will need to follow, which will come back to your lines of communication, how you manage your staff and the flexibility you are able to demonstrate when such circumstances take over the established protocols and systems.

The key here is in the clarity of your expectations and the work culture you have created, versus what seemed appropriate at a particular time. If the expression of high feelings is relatively rare in your setting then you are more likely to be better equipped to handle situations appropriately as they arise.

If on the other hand you have a work culture that is full of an atmosphere of blame, shame and complain and where it is the rule rather than the exception for staff to express themselves strongly, then you need to assess your own mode of communications and the expectations you are creating for your work place.

There are many strategies outlined in this book so far that will help you achieve this but when you know you have some difficult conversations ahead, where you expect feelings will run high, the following tips will help:

Prepare for the conversation by identifying a clear objective of what you want to achieve;

Keep that objective to yourself at the start of the conversation as the aim is to have a clear picture of the end result and what you want to happen in the future as the result of the feelings experienced up till now;

Listen and try to really understand things from the other person's perspective before expressing your own;

- Clarify your own feelings.
- Are they just about this particular situation or are they as a result of past feelings and triggers?
- Analyse what is causing those feelings and pinpoint the other person's role in contributing to them and vice versa;
- Think about the ego state these feelings are creating. Is there anything or anyone in your past that is really responsible for how you are feeling at the moment?
- Clarify how much of it is actually about the other person;

In trying to get the same clarity from the other party, ask questions that are from the adult ego state and try to keep the questions open and non-judgmental. There is great power in the simple phrase: "Tell me". Refer back to how you identified how well you listen, ask questions and give other information that we explored in chapter four. With this in mind, ask questions of the other person that will help them clarify what they are really feeling:

- What specifically do you feel angry/frustrated/disappointed/etc., about?
- Can you name the emotions and feelings?
- When else do you feel this?
- What outcome are you looking for?
- What specifically would you like me to do?
- What alternatives can you suggest that will help us both?
- What can you suggest we do differently in the future to avoid this happening again?

It is difficult to maintain the adult ego state when you are faced with some very specific behaviour, which creates either a nurturing or critical state or, a matching child state. Examples of this are when someone becomes very aggressive and throws a tantrum or dissolves easily into tears whenever confronted about their behaviour.

Coping with Tantrums

If someone becomes violent or abusive then you will want to reduce the chances of you responding angrily in turn and get out of the situation as quickly as possible. This will mean deliberately breaking any rapport so far established as you want to change the tone and outcome of the situation. Examples of how to do this include:

- Avoid strong eye contact which can increase the intensity of the emotions on both sides;
- Stand or sit at right angles to the person rather than facing them to appear less confrontational;
- Gently mirror the other's body language and movements to create a more empathetic rapport ;

Allow a little time, if you are not in any physical danger, for the other person to vent their feelings before then calmly attempting a more rational discussion. Sometimes people only wish to feel they are being listened to and that their feelings are being valued and so, once those feelings have been expressed and acknowledged, they are far more willing to engage in an adult-to-adult discussion.

Coping with Tears

There are many situations where you will expect tears from the person to whom you are talking, depending on the context of the situation and the relationship you have with them. It is in these situations that you can very clearly see how people manipulate the feelings of others to get what they want, whether they do it consciously or unconsciously.

For example, you may have a staff member that frequently fails to do what is expected and causes frustration in their colleagues. You may like this person very much or feel very protective towards them if they are particularly young or inexperienced or remind you of someone else in your life with whom you have a nurturing bond. This person may well have created behaviour to protect themselves from criticism, by playing up to their vulnerabilities and using tears as a way to evoke sympathy from others and appeal to their desire to nurture or fix them.

Invariably, this person will evoke either the critical or nurturing parent and will adapt their responses accordingly. If you sympathise and appease them they will become adaptive and compliant, giving many reasons and excuses for their behaviour and making many promises about how they will change.

Alternatively, they may become difficult, or throw a tantrum as in the example above if you strongly criticise them or use language that makes it clear that you are unhappy with them and that they are letting you down.

Neither of the above scenarios will lead to a productive conversation or outcome and this pattern may continue for months, until one or other of you explodes or the situation becomes so out of hand that other staff members start to express their dissatisfaction and you have yet more conflicts to resolve.

Again, the guidelines for preparing for such conversations are the same as some of the strategies for coping with angry tantrums. It is essential to first recognise if they are genuine or crocodile tears.

In the case of genuine tears

Stop the conversation;

Ask them if they wish to take a moment;

Empathise with how they feel;

Ask if they are able to carry on the conversation or if they would like to either take a break or reschedule for another time.

For Crocodile tears

Be aware if the other person is trying to manipulate you based on previous experiences with them or they genuinely believe themselves to be fragile and unable to cope with criticism.

If this is the case then use the above techniques as for genuine tears but resist going into parent mode and keep your tone more matter of fact and less empathetic. The purpose is to develop adult-to-adult interactions as far as possible to create the maximum *win-win* outcomes.

Giving feedback, The BOCA Model

Often, as a manager, you will have to tell people things they don't want to hear. This is always difficult, particularly if you are asking someone to change their behaviour.

Yet your aim in creating a *clearly outstanding* setting is to establish clarity about the ethos, environment and behaviour you see as *outstanding* and your communication of that. When your expectations are not met or you have to address changes then you need to be confident both in how you give and receive effective feedback.

We have already identified the need to recognise your own patterns of thoughts and behaviour and the areas where you need to be more aware of how you communicate this to others. This is the foundation for what you can expect of others.

Giving and receiving feedback for the purpose of the positive identification of areas for change and the process to get there, requires you to be extremely professional and remove, as far as possible, the personal feelings that will create adverse strong emotions or negative behaviour.

The **BOCA** process allows you to do that and to use all the communication and rapport building skills learned so far to create the most positive outcome for you, the other party and, therefore, the setting.

BOCA is a simple process that can be used in a variety of situations but is especially useful when you need to give feedback about someone's behaviour and the impact and consequences of that behaviour.

It is very useful, for example, in staff appraisals, when handling a one-off situation that has created a negative impact or, if handled correctly, for dealing with difficult parents or partners.

BOCA is an acronym that translates as:

B — Behaviour

O — Outcomes

C — Consequences

A — Actions

We have explored many examples of an emotional response to someone's behaviour, the judgements we may then place upon them according to our own map of the world and the filters we use to process external events. Very often, you will hear language being used in staff feedback situations such as:

- You must...;
- You always...;
- You should/shouldn't...;
- Your problem is...;
- Your attitude is...;
- You never...

All of the above are very inflammatory and will always bring about an emotional response. *Fight-or-flight* will come into play: defensiveness, embarrassment, lowered self-esteem to name but a few.

The Blame, Shame and Complain Game

These responses will also come about if you have a work culture made up of blame, shame and complain. How often do you hear your staff complain about the actions and behaviour of others without actually having any solutions to hand to solve whatever issue the complaint is about? Also, how often have you found that when one negative staff member who played the blame, shame complain game the loudest has been removed, they are quickly replaced by another staff member or group of staff? The original issues have not gone away but just shifted room!

Such negativity runs rampant if left unchecked and again, it is up to you as manager to set the tone for the behaviour you expect in the setting and how you manage it.

One tip (I have actually used this in a setting) is to have a money pot in the staff room and office. For a week, every time a staff member blamed, shamed or complained about someone else they had to pay a pound in to the pot. This went a great way to raising everyone's awareness of how negative the setting had become and the creation of the necessary changes then became something they all wanted rather than imposed. There was also a very tidy amount of money at the end of the week to add to the fundraising account!

This game illustrates very clearly the need to determine the cause of whatever issue is causing the problem and to focus on what can be done to change it, rather than focusing on why it went wrong in the first place. Removing the need to blame any one person in particular creates a more positive outcome for change as people will be more inclined to contribute to finding the appropriate solutions for the benefit of all.

This is the basis of the **BOCA** Model. What follows is an example of how it can be used.

Using the BOCA Model

The purpose of the model is to focus on the behaviour rather than the person. This sounds really obvious, particularly as you endeavour to apply this in how you deal with children's behaviour. Yet we do not always apply the same strategy to the adults with whom we work and wonder why subsequent behaviour and actions get worse rather than better.

An example of when to use **BOCA** is when you have to deal with a member of staff who is repeatedly late or repeatedly leaves the room they are working in, placing pressure on other staff members and attributing to an increasingly unhappy atmosphere.

You have had many staff come to you to complain about this person, using some or all of the negative phrases outlined above, and you may be feeling a mixture of frustration, embarrassment and anger at having to deal with this situation, particularly if this is not the first time it has come up. It is very difficult not to agree with what the other staff members are saying, particularly when they then demand to know the outcome of any action you may take as a result.

I once had a manager myself who point blank refused to ever disclose the outcome of complaint made, saying that as long as it was resolved it was nothing to do with anyone else. I agree up to a point. The last thing you want is a witch-hunt or staff being involved with another's performance management. However, saying nothing at all, with the situation continuing exactly as it did before, will breed frustration, resentment and only worsen the situation. The person who is the subject of the complaint may feel persecuted and the manager may lose the trust and respect of the rest of the staff.

The obvious solution is to make very clear the lines of communication and process for raising and resolving complaints. It is absolutely essential to keep the content of any such process confidential but the nature of the process is to make it clear how it will be dealt with and what the expected outcomes will be. Some communication is essential about when any action will take place and the time frame in which it will take place along with clear expectations of how the process will continue. It is not necessary to involve everyone with the reasons for the behaviour or have their input about how it should be dealt with but it must be made very clear that a process is in place and that an improvement will come about within a set timeframe.

Returning to the example of a staff member who is always late and repeatedly leaves the room the **BOCA** process would be applied as follows:

B – Identify the specific behaviour.
- What exactly is it that they are doing?
- How often?
- What is the impact on others?

Do not make it personal. It is the behaviour you are taking issue with, not the person. Also be very careful to not give examples of their behaviour based on what others have said. This will only fuel feelings of persecution and unfairness, making it feel more like a personal attack. Focus on the behaviour that you, specifically have noticed. **Use phrases like:**
- It has been brought to my attention/I have noticed that you have been late for work on several occasions and that you are frequently leaving the room.

- There are several incidences in the signing-in register and I have noticed you being out of the room up to seven times in the course of a day.
- This is having an impact on the staff ratios in the room and also on the quality of the care of the children and is not in keeping with our agreed policy and expectations.
- Can you tell me why this is happening?

This is where your preparation for tackling a potentially difficult conversation comes in. By keeping your statements factual and non-judgmental, you are allowing the other person time to reflect and to respond in a more adult way.

O – What are the outcomes or impact of the identified behaviour?

This is where you elaborate on the impact the behaviour is having on others and the setting as a whole. In this stage, you are inviting the other person to offer their explanation and raise their awareness about the impact of their behaviour. Don't assume they realise this! There could be many reasons why they are behaving as they are and by keeping things factual, adult and open, you are allowing them to explore and express why they are behaving that way without making them feel they are being persecuted.

Frequently leaving the room can often be a symptom of another, underlying issue in the room that will need to be separately addressed. Open questions and honest answers in the spirit of gaining a *win-win* outcome is the most positive action here for both parties. **Use phrases and questions such as:**

- Are you aware of how often you leave the room?
- What is happening to cause you to be late so often?
- What is happening in the room when you leave it?
- What do you consider to be the priority in the room?
- What is the atmosphere in the room like when you return?
- What happens when you are in the room and it is short-staffed?
- I appreciate how much you do in the room but the impact of you not being there enough is...

C – Identify and express the specific consequences of the behaviour

You have already commented on the impact on others and referred to the agreed policy and expectations that are not being adhered to. Now you need to be specific about what will happen if the behaviour continues. Again, keep it factual and not personal and allow the person to remain in adult state by asking for their input and agreement about the impact their behaviour is having. Building on the answers to the questions above, use phrases and questions such as:

- Are you aware of our policy on lateness?
- What do you feel is the impact of someone leaving the room regularly?
- How do you feel this impacts on the other staff members?
- What else is happening?
- I appreciate you may not have been aware.....

These questions should allow the other person to demonstrate their knowledge of the systems in place and allow you to decide the best course of action.

- Are they genuinely unaware of the impact of their behaviour and the explicit policies and expectations on lateness and staff ratios?
- Are there underlying issues in the room that need to be addressed?
- Are there other areas of their performance that you are unhappy with?
- Are there specific, external reasons for their lateness that can be addressed?

The final part of the process is:

A – What actions are you specifically going to take to resolve the issue?

This is where you want to gain agreement with the other party about the best course of action to resolve the issue. Thinking back to how we react when we are faced with criticism, whether we feel it is justified or not, the key here is to empower the other person to make their own decision and take responsibility for the agreed actions. Otherwise you run the risk of the person agreeing with you but inwardly feeling very resentful and upset leading them to not only continue with the original behaviour but also start demonstrating other behavioural issues that have an even more negative impact.

Involving the other party – ask questions and use phrases such as

- What options are there for you to make sure you arrive to work on time?
- What do you need from me to make that happen?
- Shall we look through the policy and role expectations together so you can be clear about why we have them and for me to understand your interpretation of them?
- What will you do to make sure you minimise the number of times that you leave the room?
- How shall we monitor this?

- Shall we agree to meet again in two weeks to discuss progress and any other options?

By putting the onus on the other person to come up with solutions and offering your support, you are far more likely to get them to stick to any agreed outcomes. Also, being clear about an agreed monitoring period keeps things professional and allows the other person to know that you expect things to improve within an agreed time. It also means that other staff members can see that changes are being made without necessarily having to know the reasons for the behaviour in the first place.

Reflecting on your own behaviour

In situations such as these it may well be that some of the reasons for the behaviour of your member of staff are as a result of your own behaviour. For example, you may have neglected to make clear the staff policy and expectations or allowed other staff members to regularly be late due to personal reasons. If this is the case, and if any faults on your part are raised by the other party, then it is essential that you remain in adult state and model the behaviour you expect.

Keep your tone neutral and try to avoid any defensive reaction. You can then choose to accept the criticism and take responsibility for your actions by apologising and giving assurances that things will be done differently in future. This will demonstrate your own honesty and integrity as well as your own willingness to learn from feedback and make appropriate changes.

Alternatively, if you feel the criticism is unjustified then you can disagree but keep the conversation emotion free by not making counter accusations, deferring the topic till another time or focussing on other aspects of the conversation to continue to move forwards.

Summary

This chapter has provided you with tips and strategies for giving feedback that allows for more positive outcomes for you, your staff and your setting.

The next chapter looks at how you can use these tools to be more flexible in your day to day management through the identification and effective delegation of specific tasks to free your own time and develop the skills and capabilities of your staff.

Blank BOCA Model

This is a useful format to use when having to give feedback in a variety of situations. The process places emphasis on the behaviour and actions of the person and not on the person themselves. It is therefore much easier to create and maintain an adult-to-adult rapport and conversation.

B: Behaviour

- What is the specific behaviour that need to be addressed?
- What is happening, how often and to whom, if relevant?

O: Outcomes

- What are the specific consequences of the behaviour?
- Who is being affected?
- How is the behaviour impacting on the setting?

C: Consequences

- What are the specific consequences if the behaviour were to continue?
- What does this mean in relation to agreed job specifications, expectations, action plans?

A: Actions

- What will happen now?
- What specific actions will be taken and by whom?
- How will these actions be monitored?

An example situation using BOCA

A member of staff was consistently late for work. As room leader, it was their responsibility to be in the room when parents and children first arrived. The manager was reluctant to make an issue as it was only a matter of a few minutes lateness but the increasing impact on other staff members prompted action. The **BOCA** model was used as follows:

Behaviour:

I have noticed that there have been several occasions when the expected number and members of staff are not in the room at the appointed time. What is your view on this?

Outcomes:

The outcomes of this is that; parents are not being greeted by the appropriate staff members; the room is not set up properly and is not properly welcoming for the children; other staff are having to come in earlier to compensate.

Consequences:

The consequence, if this behaviour were to continue, is a re-evaluation of job role and specifications, within a formal meeting.

Actions:

Discussion about causes of the behaviour and suggestions from staff member about what will happen and why such as:

• Room leader to ensure presence in room five minutes before parents and children arrive.

• Room leader to monitor the rota of other staff.

- Re-evaluation of job spec and expectations, to accommodate any necessary changes in the rota.

Obviously, the conversation would not be this stilted but the process allows for focus to be placed, not on blaming and complaining, but in the calm discussion of facts and possible solutions.

9. THE ART OF GOOD DELEGATION

THE WHOLE PURPOSE OF THIS book has been to challenge you to consider your thoughts and behaviour and determine if they are working well in getting you to your intended end result. By examining what you do in terms of your beliefs and values, the ways you filter your experiences and how you choose to respond and communicate with others, you have been able to assess what changes you need to make and to develop the necessary knowledge, skills and strategies to make it happen.

Now you have clarified your vision of *outstanding*, identified the changes you need to make and studied the various strategies and tools that can help you, it is now time to put them all in the context of being flexible.

I have often said to managers with whom I have worked, that clarity is the first step; establishing the relevant systems and procedures and creating consistency in their use is the second; and being able to reflect, adapt and demonstrate flexibility is the third.

The more knowledge you gain about yourself and others around you, the more you have the ability to

222

adapt your systems and behaviour without losing focus on the end result.

The manager's lack of confidence to do that, is one of the most frequent reasons that different Early Years settings flounder and why they feel intimidated by the changes and advice being constantly thrown at them by external agencies or Ofsted. Knowing what you want, what you have to do and managing your communication to build an effective rapport with the people you need, is the key to creating a *clearly outstanding* setting.

This chapter focuses on how to delegate effectively to get the best intended outcome. It draws upon the need for you to be clear and then commit to the actions you decide to take, while also staying aware of your own level of responsibility and the responsibility you are encouraging others to take.

At the end of this chapter you will find an example of the key points to consider when delegating, using a contextual example.

Understanding what delegation is

I get mixed responses during training courses when the word delegation comes up. Some managers nod wisely as we discuss what good delegation is, while others look at me as though I have landed from another planet.

The reasons for this are varied. Some settings are very restricted in terms of number of staff or have only one manager, who has responsibility for everything, making it very difficult to delegate any of the workload. Some settings have a management team who are able to share responsibilities and tasks.

In all settings however, there is definitely the opportunity to delegate when it comes to implementing the systems you have put in place. This includes the way you choose to manage your staff and also how you encourage your room leaders, in particular, to manage the practitioners in their individual rooms.

Whatever the individual set-up of your setting, the following questions can help you identify where the potential exists to increase delegation.

Delegating specific tasks

Is there someone who can do the task better than you? Are there skill sets or knowledge within your team or staff that you are not really tapping in to at the moment? For example, is there:

Someone who has more specific knowledge of special needs or other specific training that can help shape the curriculum you deliver?

Someone who has slightly more time than you and could do the task to a good standard even if it is in a slightly different way than you would do it. For example, a deputy or administrator if one is available? Someone who is paid less than you that could do the task satisfactorily, e.g., putting up displays, ordering resources and so on, who would be more cost-effective than you?

Someone who would benefit from doing the task as part of their on-going professional development, e.g., a room leader who would like to take on more mentoring responsibility or would like to have more responsibility for monitoring or planning?

I appreciate that potential barriers to any or all of the above include lack of paid time to take on such tasks and the already long working hours of some staff, who do not wish to take on additional responsibility when there is no additional financial reward.

This again comes back to your clarity of expectations and how much trust and mutual goodwill you have created in your setting. In the recruitment and retention of your staff for example, while you may not be able to offer higher wages, you may be able to offer opportunities to build on skills and passions of individual staff members that can be acknowledged through continuous professional development and recognition to others.

However, if the answer to any of the above questions is "yes", then there is the opportunity to delegate. You may well think that you already use the opportunity to delegate but still find yourself in a situation where what you wanted to happen didn't or the task took far longer than expected or worse, didn't happen at all.

A common example is where a room leader will ask a member of staff to create a display. Three weeks later, the display has not even been started, only half done, or not as the room leader expected it to be. The room leader will feel angry and frustrated and the staff member to whom the task was delegated, may feel confused and upset at the negative feedback their efforts have caused.

Usually, this is the result of the nature of the task or the time frame for completion not being set-out clearly enough, or a lack of discussion about potential obstacles that may prevent the task from being completed. Also, assumptions play a great part here. It is very easy to assume that just because you work in the same room together you will all have the same idea for how things should look or what should be expected or what constitutes a priority.

Again, this goes back to you, as a manager, being clear about what you expect to see, hear and feel in each room and how effectively you have communicated this to your staff. Have you established clear job roles, responsibilities, expectations and the systems to monitor them?

Are you an effective delegator and do you create the right environment and process to enable your staff to effectively delegate to others?

There are many reasons why it is important to delegate to help you create the desired end result and be *clearly outstanding*. Equally, there are many reasons why so many people find it difficult to do.

Reasons to delegate

- To allow you more time to concentrate on more high priority work;
- To develop other people's skills;
- To help people learn from the experience;
- To motivate people by making them valued;
- To help develop your own working relationship with individual team and staff members;
- To learn more about the specific knowledge and skills set of individual staff;
- To ensure an even spread of work load and responsibility across all staff;
- To protect yourself and the setting, knowing that everything in the setting will run smoothly in your absence.

However, some managers still find the process of delegation difficult.

Reasons that people choose not to delegate

- An unwillingness to lose control and let go of overall responsibility;
- Lack of confidence in the people who work with and for you;
- Fear that someone else might actually do it better and you will feel undermined;
- Feeling superior, that no one else could possibly do the task better than you;
- Enjoyment of feeling overworked and indispensable;
- Lack of training, not knowing how to effectively delegate;
- Not having anyone in place to whom you can delegate;

I have seen many of those reasons displayed in managers and staff with whom I have worked but without exception, they were unaware of the negative impact their behaviour was having and truly believed they were doing the right thing. In the case of the last point, having no-one to whom you can delegate is a tough one. This requires you to return to the creation of your vision for the setting. What exactly is it you want to achieve? What are the steps you need to take to make that happen? What changes need to be made and who is responsible for making them?

To Delegate or Not to Delegate?

Frequently, the issues that arise around the way to delegate come about because it is not always clear what is, or isn't, appropriate to delegate. Frequent confusion, misunderstanding and even complete breakdowns in communication and relationships come about due to the nature of the task being delegated and the reasons behind it.

Tasks that are appropriate to delegate are

- Routine tasks, such as administration tasks, putting up displays, organising resources etc;
- Whole tasks – this means a specific project like taking on the recording and delivery of physical activities such as Sticky Kids or Top Tots;
- Tasks that someone else can do much better or more cheaply, such as responsibility for co-ordinating messy play and craft activities, financial tasks, special needs resources and delivery, writing parent newsletters;
- Tasks planned for the future with no pressing deadline, for example fundraising events, in-house training, specific activities for the children, changing resources or a room layout, displays;
- Tasks carried out at regular intervals, such as administration tasks, updating records, invoices, meeting with parents, monitoring of specific areas that are then reported back to you to oversee.

Tasks that are not appropriate to delegate include

- Anything that has accountability that should stay with you. For example, staff appraisals, dealing with specific complaints, meeting with external advisors or trainers that will involve decision making for the whole setting, making and writing policies, staff handbooks or any communication that is representing the vision, ethos, values and actions of the setting;

- New tasks that require the gaining of new knowledge and skills that you, as manager, need to be aware of;

- Tasks that you simply don't like doing for that very reason. Nothing creates resentment quicker in the people to whom you delegate;

- Tasks that have been specifically delegated to you, as the manager, from Board members, Ofsted or other external advisors;

- Critical tasks where failure would cause huge problems. For example staff disciplinaries, interviewing new staff, dealing with parent complaints, creating new policies or systems.

Finally, the two things to always avoid are dumping and abdicating responsibility. Both of these are indicators of poor management and will not help you in your aim to effectively communicate your own and the setting's ethos, values and behaviour. In your quest to continually develop good rapport and communication with your staff, any actions that involve dumping or advocating any of your personal responsibility will quickly add to any communication or poor team-work issues you have already identified in your setting.

Steps to create good delegation

As with good communication, the purpose of delegation is to gain a positive outcome. The whole point is to free-up your time as manager to focus on other priorities, secure in the knowledge that what you delegate will not only be done well but will jointly benefit you and the person to whom you delegated the task.

The following list outlines the main steps when preparing to delegate tasks

- Identify exactly what you want done and the specific time frame in which you would like it completed;
- Identify the level of responsibility and authority to be delegated for the task and how you will communicate this to the relevant person or people;
- Identify the appropriate and necessary levels of knowledge, skills, attitude and experience required

by the person or people to whom you are delegating;

- Identify any potential barriers to the successful completion of the task within the identified time frame;

- List the phases of the delegation process, with a brief description of each phase and your clear expectations of what you expect to see within the specific time frames;

- Identify how you will monitor the delegated task. Provide examples that could be set as specific measures at each identified stage and completion of the task.

The above steps are broad indicators of what to consider when delegating. Below is a specific, ten-point process that I will put into a contextual example to illustrate its most effective use:

Delegation — A Ten Point Process
1. Identify the task

- What exactly is it you want to delegate?
- Is it all of the task or only part of it?
- Let's say you want to create a new parent information display board. First of all you need to be very clear about:
    o How you want the board to look;
    o The information it is to contain;

o How often it is to be changed and updated;

o Of which parts you specifically wish to retain control, for example the displaying of the setting Development Plan or specific notices that you want to bring to parents' attention;

o For which parts you are happy to delegate responsibility, for example the colours used, the way information is laid out.

2. Identify the right person for the task

What experience level does the task need? Can you spread the task and the responsibility to involve more people and avoid issues of favouritism or are there other tasks they could do instead? What skill level do they need? How much discussion and coaching time to you need to give versus the actual time you have? For something as creative as a display then it makes sense to involve someone who has a proven track record of producing good displays and already has an understanding for how you like things to look. Depending on how much control you are willing to relinquish, you may opt to give only a broad outline for the finished result and trust the details to the person to whom you have chosen to delegate.

However, it is vital that you are still very clear about what you expect and how much creative license you are granting, as there is nothing worse than saying to someone to carry out the task as they see fit, only to later criticise their efforts because the finished result was not how you imagined it to be.

If the board is to be changed on a regular basis consider how others can be involved. For example, you may be including a section that shows photos of the children in their play or examples of their work. If this is the case and there is a clearly demarcated space for such items then you may wish to delegate to each room leader the task of filling the space at regular intervals as they see fit.

If you are choosing to use this task as a way of developing the skills and experience of a new or inexperienced staff member, then you will need to consider how much time you will need to spend with them to fully explain your expectations and how you will monitor their progress.

3. Explain why you are delegating it to them

Sell it to them! What is in it for them? Will it show how much you value their input? Will it develop their skills and experience? What will they be able to do as a result of the task? Is it a skill to add to their portfolio? An example of taking on responsibility?

Be very clear about how much you will appreciate them completing the task and how it is benefitting the setting as a whole.

We have already covered the golden rule of never dumping or abdicating responsibility when delegating and you equally have to be careful of how you communicate your reasons for delegating. It is essential to get across authenticity and genuine mutual benefit if you are to gain the most positive outcome and build on the successful practice and relationships that contribute to being *clearly outstanding*.

4. Specify the expected outcomes

What will the completed task look like? It is vitally important and goes back to beginning with the end in mind. In this example, what is the purpose of the display? Who will see it? How will it benefit the people who look at it? What message do you want it to give to parents and outside visitors about what happens in your setting and the response you wish to receive?

Thinking about these questions in advance will make it much easier to select and explain to the chosen person to whom you are delegating and will reduce the risk of confusion and frustration if things don't go to plan.

5. Establish a specific finish date

Agree the completion date and gain the other party's input about how long they feel it will realistically take to complete.

This often trips-up managers and room leaders. You may think you have been clear but unless you specifically state the time frame, the phrase "as soon as possible" can be interpreted by some to mean immediately, by others to mean the end of the day and by others to mean when they can get round to it. Use very specific language and be sure both parties are in complete agreement about the time frame and the level of priority the task is to take.

6. Discuss how it will be done

Ask the person to whom you are delegating how they feel they can best achieve the outcome. This empowers them to consider the time and resources they have and to be more committed to the process because it has stemmed from their own input.

7. Identify the required resources

- How much time it will take? Is the task to be carried out during the normal working day or outside of it?
- Will finding the time have an impact on anyone else? For example, if they are to come out of the room to complete the task will you provide cover for them or will other staff members have to shoulder some additional responsibility while the task is being completed?

- Equipment and resources. Are the necessary resources available or will they have to be bought in? Will the person completing the task have to use any tools or resources that are also required by others?
- Money. Is there a budget required?
- People. Does anyone else need to be involved? Is there anyone else who can help them, e.g., a student or apprentice?

8. Decide how and when you are going to monitor progress

This depends on the complexity of the task, what risk there is of things going wrong and the possible consequences.

You need to highlight specific stages of review.

In this example, if you have agreed on a week to complete the task, you may want to arrange a review of progress after three days. This will allow you to identify any obstacles that are preventing the task being completed and put in further steps and resources to overcome them.

9. Identify who else needs to be informed

- Other managers or room leaders;
- The team itself to avoid any confusion, wrong assumptions or gossip about what they are doing and why;

- Other involved parties, such as Board members, parents (via newsletters). Has it been entered on the Development Plan or Self Evaluation Document for Ofsted?

10. Check list to see if the delegation was a success

In the spirit of continually reflecting upon and improving your practice, it is useful to have some criteria by which to measure your success and identify areas for improvement. This also helps build rapport and successful relationships, as it offers the opportunity to praise a job well done or identify any gaps in the knowledge or skills of individuals that you can improve with training.

Most importantly, it creates and maintains a two way process for the future. When people feel truly valued and achieve success on their own merits, they are more willing to repeat the experience and offer their services again. This creates a *win-win* situation because the more you know the more you can do – the stronger the relationship, the more flexibility of behaviour can be implemented to create the best possible outcomes (see success checklist at end of chapter).

Summary

This has been a very specific chapter to provide clear strategies to recognise where delegation can be beneficial and explain the use of specific tools that help create good delegation in your setting.

At the end of this chapter I have included further examples of delegated tasks within settings that have been highlighted as difficult, such as delegating monitoring within rooms and assigning specific tasks to practitioners.

The next chapter focuses on time management and where you can develop more clarity about your priorities and the systems needed to get more done, as well as the necessary flexibility to cope with day to day changes.

Delegation Check List, Success Checklist and Contextual Example

Below is a clear check list to use when you or one of your staff need to delegate. On the following page I have used the checklist to provide a specific example of delegating a monitoring task.

Delegation — A Ten-Point Process
1. Identify the task

• Decide what should be delegated, be specific.

• All of the task or part of it?

2. Identify the right person

- What is their level of experience?
- Are you making sure to vary the people to whom you delegate tasks, to avoid favouritism and promote fair practice?
- What is the required skill level for the task?
- How much coaching/training input will be required versus how much time you actually have to do so?

3. Explain why you are delegating it to them

- Sell it to them, why should they do it?
- What benefits will it bring?
- What will they be able to do as a result of it?
- Tell them how appreciative you will be.

4. Specify the expected outcomes

- What will the completed task look like?
- What will be done as a result?

5. Establish a target completion date

- Agree the target. Ask them how long it will take so you can negotiate a realistic time frame.
- Will it be a one-off piece of time required or will it be ongoing?
- How will progress be monitored?

6. Discuss how

- Ask them how they feel they can tackle it. Encouraging their input gets more buy-in.

7. Identify the resources required

- Time – will they have to be taken away from other responsibilities? Do you need cover staff?
- Equipment and resources;
- Money — will a budget be required or will funds need to be available for cover staff?
- People — who else can help them?

8. Decide how and when you are going to monitor progress

- Depends on the complexity of task, the potential risk of it going wrong and the subsequent consequences.
- May need to highlight milestones to review, for example on a weekly basis.

9. Identify who else needs to be informed

- The rest of the staff to avoid any misunderstanding, gossip or assumptions.
- Other parties such as parents or Board members if the task requires input from them, for example in completing questionnaires for monitoring purposes.

10. Feedback on the results

- Use the following success checklist to identify the success level and necessary next steps.

Delegation Success Checklist

Following the completion of the delegated task, discuss the outcome with the delegate. This gives you the opportunity to praise a job well done, build rapport and trust and also assess the development that has taken place.

It also provides an opportunity for future development. By empowering your staff they will be more willing to take on-board additional responsibilities that will move you further towards your goal of being *clearly outstanding*.

Use the following checklist

- Was the task completed as agreed?
- How well has it been done?
- What needs to be done to correct any shortcomings revealed?
- Was the initial brief good enough?
- Was the right person chosen?
- Were all resources readily available?
- Did the work provide sufficient challenge?
- Was the work too difficult for the delegate? Why?
- What has the delegate contributed creatively, on top of the requirement to perform proficiently?

• What lessons have been learned for the future?

What next?

Using the checklists to delegate a monitoring task

Monitoring is often a task that is delegated within a setting, usually by the manager as part of the continuous professional development of a deputy manager or room leader. However, it is often an area that causes much confusion.

Questions to ask as part of the delegation process include

• What, specifically do I want to be monitored?
• Why do I want it to be monitored?
• How often and for how long?
• What will happen as a result of the monitoring?

Just delegating the monitoring of use of resources or outside play is a very broad theme. Without the specifics of what is being monitored, why it is being monitored and what is going to happen as a result of the monitoring, the delegation process can often be misunderstood and create confusion and frustration when things don't appear to change or improve.

With this in mind, the checklist can be used as follows

* Define the task:

   What, specifically is it you want to monitor? Is it use of the outside area in terms of frequency, how the area is set up, evidence of activities in the planning or use of specific equipment for example? Is the person to whom you are delegating responsible for the whole task or only part of it? How much are you going to do if at all?

* Select the individual:

   Who is the most suitable person for the job? Is it your deputy or a room leader or a trainee? What experience/skill levels do they have? How much support time will you have to provide? Why delegate to them? Have they requested more responsibility? What is the mutual benefit of delegating the task to them? Does the person or people selected have the right level of ability to do the task? Is it something they have done before or will they require a certain amount of input/training/support from you as part of the process? Is it something you will do together at first?

- Explain the reasons:
  Why are you choosing this person or people in particular? Is it linked to action points from their appraisal? Is it part of other identified areas of continuous professional development? Is it to give them a level of responsibility as part of a new role? Is it part of a training exercise?

- State the required results:
  What, specifically, is the evidence you wish to see when the task is completed? How exactly do you want them to complete the task? Are you giving any opportunity for them to use their own initiative in determining the process providing the end result is clearly met? How can you get their buy-in? How certain are you that both parties have the same understanding of the desired end result and that both are happy to proceed? For example, if the task is to monitor weekly planning, you need to identify in which aspects of the planning you are specifically interested. For example, is it for evidence of sustained shared thinking activities, or use of role play? How is the evidence of this going to be collated and presented?

- Agree the deadlines:
  Over what period of time is the monitoring to take place? How often will it take place? What time will

245

be given for the information to be gathered and presented? Will the results be used to inform Board members or parents? Is part of the delegated task to feedback the findings in a staff meeting? Is there a specific future date in mind?

- Discuss how the task will be carried out:
  What are their ideas for how the task should be carried out? How well does this fit with your desired end result? Are there areas where you can compromise without losing the purpose behind the task and the desired outcome?

- Consider the resources required:
  This can include concrete resources such as books, pens, folders etc. It can also mean the resource of time and involvement of other staff members. Will they be given specified time out of the room to complete the task? If so, how often will this be and what needs to be put in place to cover them if necessary?

- How and when will progress be monitored:
  How often will you meet to discuss progress and to identify any barriers or obstacles that may have come up? What effect may these have on the agreed timeline?

- Support and communicate; who else needs to know?:

  What support level have you agreed? Who else needs to be informed and taken into consideration? What effect will the monitoring have on other staff members or the children? Have you explained the purpose of the monitoring and what will happen as a result? Are there ways to include and value the input of other staff as well as of the delegate?

Use the success checklist to feedback on results. Define the success of the task and what will happen now as a result of it.

10. MANAGING YOUR TIME

Understanding and identifying how to prioritise

THE MOST COMMON COMPLAINT I hear from managers is that there is simply not enough time in the day to get things done. Fire-fighting a-plenty goes on every day as a way of coping with the continuous demands and sheer volume of tasks that need to get done.

Managing your time effectively is not easy and will also depend very much on your own personal strategies. Some people thrive under pressure and are able to multi-task without breaking a sweat, appearing to achieve the impossible. Others struggle to cope with organising a daily routine for themselves let alone for anyone else and frequently become stressed or ill when faced with increasing pressure.

In my experience, the more stressed the manager, the more stressed is the whole working environment and the more incidents there are of chaos, disruption and examples of poor performance. The premise throughout this book is to recognise the necessity of making and sustaining change from the top down as it is up to you, as managers and owners, to lead by example and create the attitudes, behaviour and environment you wish others to follow.

It is so easy to feel and become overwhelmed and also not unusual for managers to frequently put in very long hours, with no extra pay or recognition and at the expense of their personal life. While there is no magic formula to make the role easier or better compensated financially, there are ways to change your current habits and actions to create more positive and sustainable changes.

This chapter will look at specific strategies and tools to help you:

- Identify exactly what it is you need to do;
- Explore the reasons you find for not doing them;
- Prioritise your activities;
- Create the right systems to ensure things get done;
- Identify where you can choose to delegate;
- Use your rapport building and communication skills to learn to say no to others.

The art of choosing your priorities

How we choose to spend our time depends on what priority we place on different tasks and how easily we allow ourselves to be distracted. Manager's tasks are often prioritised on their immediate urgency, rather than their importance.

This is what leads to the fire-fighting mentality and is one of the main reasons that, despite having the best intentions and clearly defined action plans and lists, the important tasks that will benefit the setting in the long-term, tend to be put aside in favour of dealing with what is immediately presented.

The truth is that there are very few tasks that are both urgent and important despite how they may appear or how someone else is trying to present them. The obvious exceptions are, of course, an Ofsted visit, accident in the work place or other incident that will cause immediate disruption to routines. However, we tend to get drawn into thinking, according to other people's agenda and how persuasive they are, that tasks are more urgent or important than is actually the case.

Equally, it is very common for managers to start out with a clear plan of action and a specific list of things to get done, only to then be distracted by sudden emergencies or the demands made by others, in which case the list goes out the window, frequently along with the manager's sanity!

The ability to keep your focus by understanding the difference between urgent and important, requires you to return to the premise of beginning with the end in mind. If you have made sure that you have established your vision for your setting, how you communicate that vision, the resources and staff you have put in place and the behaviour you expect to achieve it, then it is far easier to incorporate what is a priority in your subsequent Development or Action Plans.

Becoming aware of barriers to time management

Yet time and time again, if you will excuse the expression, those plans are not followed, despite the best of intentions. Some of the reasons for this are listed below:

- New changes are imposed by external agencies or Ofsted that mean previous plans are no longer relevant;
- You have identified, as part of your own desire to be more self-aware, that you do not like saying "no" to others or find it difficult to delegate, both of which we have addressed in previous chapters;
- You hold a genuine, long-held and often unconscious belief that you are by nature a very poor time manager;
- You feel overwhelmed by all you have to do and will deploy various tactics to avoid what you know you have to do;
- You genuinely do not know where to begin and lack the knowledge or skills to create a clear plan that will help you feel confident to prioritise your activities and communicate your reasons for doing so to others.

Everyone, at some time or another and to a greater or lesser degree, finds it difficult to manage their time and will happily distract themselves with trivial pursuits as a way to avoid them. As we have already identified, to be *clearly outstanding* requires you to have (and communicate) absolute clarity about the things that are really important to you and to then develop all the knowledge, skills and capabilities to help you achieve them.

Part of this process involves developing the confidence to engage with others and to respond to their requests or demands. This means seeking guidance to help determine how well what is being advised or asked for, actually suits your identified priorities and aims for the setting.

It is therefore essential, when appropriate, to say "no" to apparently urgent things that come up and remain focused on what you have identified as important.

Example

An example of this would be where you have identified the need to carry out staff appraisals and review your current job descriptions and role responsibilities. The purpose of this is to really assess all the skills and resources you have and to implement any changes in staff ratios, hours worked, training or re-deployment that you have identified as necessary to achieve the best quality care and service for your setting.

To do this effectively will require a great deal of forward planning, particularly if you work in a setting where a separate, private room is not always readily available. You may need to liaise with other staff or any external visitors who also need the room and to then place it very firmly in the diary.

I have known many managers who have done this and then found various events take over that result in the appraisals being deferred for days, weeks or even months.

The effect of this is to create an environment where you feel you are always chasing your tail, while the issues you sought to address by having the appraisals not only get worse but may then become a catalyst for other problems.

Identifying the solutions

First of all it useful to make the distinction between what is important and what is urgent. If we define activities or tasks that are important as being those that are likely to have a major impact or long-term benefit then examples may include the following:

- Long-term goal setting and planning;
- Funding and grant applications;
- Staff reviews and appraisals;
- Creating or updating websites and other literature such as prospectuses and handbooks;
- Reviewing and updating policies;
- Meetings with partnership agencies and external advisors;

253

- Training;
- Review and updates on staff handbooks and training manuals;
- Parent meetings;
- Staff meetings;
- Review of job descriptions and setting expectations;
- Essential administrations such as invoices and data handling;
- Monitoring of staff performance, planning and assessment procedures;
- Time away from the setting for personal reflection and planning;
- Relationship building and networking;
- Delegation;
- Developing your own knowledge, capabilities and skills;
- Personal development.

Similarly, tasks and activities that can be defined as urgent and needing immediate attention may include:

- Crises management, staff absence or accidents;
- Important deadlines such as preparing for an inspection;
- Fire-fighting activities such as invoice payments, parent visits, visits from advisors or other partnership agencies.

The list of important activities may vary in the sense of how urgent you think they are and where they are on your priority list. Similarly, time spent fire-fighting could be reduced if planning and systems are put in place as part of the priorities for what you consider to be important.

All activities are either urgent, important or a mixture of both. It really is a personal choice about how you interpret them and respond to them but raising your awareness of how you are choosing to spend most of your time and how effective that is in achieving your long-term goal, is essential to keep you properly focused on your desired outcomes.

Tips to help you recognise how to prioritise using the urgent v important method include:

- Recognising that very few tasks are both urgent and important;
- Important tasks often only get done when they become urgent;
- Urgent tasks appear to be important because they seem to require immediate action but may not actually be important in terms of how they will help you achieve your long-term goal;
- By constantly dealing with urgent tasks all the time or fire fighting, long-term goals may get continually put off;

- You find yourself always racing against the clock rather than having a clear sense of purpose and direction.

Below is an example of the matrix I have used in my training sessions. This comes from the author Stephen R Covey, in his book, *The Seven Habits of Highly Effective People*.

Covey uses this matrix to demonstrate how we tend to divide our time and what types of activity we choose to focus on. I have inserted some of the examples from the above lists:

	High Urgency	**Low Urgency**
High Importance	Crises management Fire-fighting Important deadlines	Planning Thinking space Personal development Relationship building and networking Delegation
Low Importance	Interruptions Phone calls E-mails Other people's agenda Too many meetings	Time wasters and chatters in the office! Avoidance Procrastination — finding anything to do except what you are supposed to

If you are anything like me while I was writing this book, you could add several other items to the list of low importance and low urgency activities. My cupboards have never been so clean and tidy or my paperwork so neatly organised. It was also amazing how suddenly I had all the time in the world to answer requests from friends and family and e-mail long lost buddies.

It is interesting how all the excuses with which managers come prepared, fall away when they look at this matrix during my training courses. This is especially the case when I ask them to fill in the matrix using examples of how they spend a typical week. I have included a blank copy of this matrix in the resource section at the end of the chapter for you to try this.

It is also a real eye-opener when managers realise how many interruptions they get from staff because they have been trying to have an open door policy. Being approachable is an excellent idea but it is also essential that you allow the time to complete your identified tasks and the door can certainly be open but not necessarily all the time.

Spotting time wasters and tips to avoid them

One manager I know had a variety of fun signs that she put on her door according to how much or little she wanted to be disturbed. Deliberately making the signs humorous and varying when she used them gave a clear message to her staff; that they were very important but so was her time.

Further tips are:

- Look carefully at the systems and rotas you have in place. If staff are constantly coming into the office rather than being in the room, what isn't working?
- Have clear expectations for how long different conversations may take. Sharing an office inevitably means there will be a certain amount of conversation and banter that is not work related but it is possible to put time restrictions on them. Create an agreement on break and chat times so you can focus on what you need to do.
- There is an expression in business that if your desk is full of work frogs, then swallow the biggest one first. Continually focusing on the smaller tasks and avoiding the main one that will have a more long-term positive impact will only make you fall further behind and create more issues to overcome.
- Think about the space and room availability in your setting. If your office is also the main point of contact for parents coming in then structure your day so you can tackle certain activities when it is quieter.

- If you have constant phone calls, block out an hour of time when it is reasonable to do so and allow the answer machine to pick up if no-one else is available. You can check the machine at regular intervals in case you miss anything urgent but if you do not put value on your time you can be assured that no one else will.

- Create specific times when staff may come in to request information or for booking time off or checking other information that requires your input.

- If staff do not actually need to speak to you, avoid the temptation to chat with them by using a sign on the day saying something like, "Come in, do your thing but don't be offended if I don't talk to you!"

- Similarly, if there are phone calls that other staff answer, request that they don't disturb you but take a message instead and inform you at a later, more convenient time unless it is an emergency. Make very clear here exactly what you define as being an emergency to avoid any confusion and further interruptions.

As always, be clear about what specifically you want and how you can most effectively communicate it. Once you realise how much time you are spending in each quadrant and how this is either moving you further towards (or away from) your goals and plans, it becomes easier to refocus on your original priorities and vision for your setting.

If having a *clearly outstanding* setting means, for example, having well-qualified and motivated staff and clear systems in place for communication, planning and assessment, then it becomes easier to say "no" to distractions that will steer you away from that.

The excuse of having no time for something is in direct proportion to how important that activity is to you and your goals. Think, for example, of people who say they would like to lose weight and exercise more. They may draw up a detailed plan of exactly what they want to do and how they are going to do it and start out with great enthusiasm. A week in, however, and most of those plans have gone by the wayside. Invitations to eat out, bad weather and other distractions soon weaken the resolve and it is much easier to say they will start again in the New Year or when the weather is nicer.

Compare this to a family member or friend falling ill and needing regular hospital visits. Somehow, everything else becomes less important and there is no question about finding the time to make a daily visit.

This is why it is so important to do things that fit in with your values and beliefs. If something is truly important to you, you will go the extra mile to make sure things get done. Time is not an issue because you choose to minimise the amount of distractions you allow to take you away from your focus.

Having the confidence to know what you want and being focused on achieving it, is all the more powerful if you also allow yourself to be flexible. This means you are prepared to stay more open to external events or people that may benefit your long-term goal and introduce you to other ways of thinking and doing things that are more effective.

With this confidence also comes the ability to consider the views and requests of others and feel comfortable about saying "no" if those requests do not fit with your values, ethos and current aims and priorities.

The Art of saying "No"

In the chapter on tackling difficult conversations we looked at the various reasons we have for choosing to avoid confronting certain issues. Choosing to say "no" and having the ability and confidence to do so is certainly one of them.

The bottom line is, if you do not value your own time and do not make it clear by your behaviour that this is the case, then you leave yourself wide open for others to take advantage of that and distract you with their own agenda. Equally, if you are trying to create an efficient and well-motivated staff then you need to lead by example.

If staff constantly see you doing everything else but what you have said you are going to do and also hear you complaining about never having enough time, then you are effectively creating a blueprint for how you expect them to say and do the same. This is particularly the case if you are consistently failing to follow through on promises you have made to deal with certain issues or make identified changes.

Whatever you say you are going to do, you need to commit to it. If you find you are constantly making excuses for letting others down, then you need to look carefully at how realistic those commitments are and how much you truly value them.

Again, clarity comes before commitment. Flexibility can be created if changes need to occur, by taking appropriate ownership and responsibility for those changes and taking into consideration their effect on others. This will then show your staff that you can be trusted and that you value them, which will foster similar behaviour and actions in them.

You may also be frequently put in the position where external advisors and partners are putting demands on you. It is very tempting to try and accommodate everyone's wishes for the sake of keeping smooth relationships or to keep access to funding or resources as a result. However, you run the risk of becoming overwhelmed and losing your focus about what it is you are really trying to achieve.

Commitment and consistency

When faced with situations such as these, either by staff members or external parties, use the following guide to decide how much time you need to give to the request and how much it will benefit you and your setting:

From your staff

- Is the request reasonable and is it something that lies within your control?
- Is it something that needs to be done straightaway or can it be dealt with at a later time or by someone else?
- Is it something you have already put off several times and are now running the risk of damaging the professional relationship with the person making the request?
- Does the request or the time it will take fit in with the agreed long-term goals, policies and expectations you have in place?

From people outside the setting

- Is the request being made by Ofsted, in which case saying "no" is probably not an option!
- Is the request being made as part of your agreed contractual obligation to the person or people asking? We looked at this in detail in chapter four, the importance of knowing exactly where you stand

in terms of what you are obligated, as opposed to advised, to do.

- Does the request fit into your existing systems and policies?
- Are you confident that you can strongly evidence a refusal of the request on the grounds that what you already do is working well?
- Is the request or suggestion something that could add further value to what you already do?
- Will the request be manageable given your existing workload and priorities?

In both respects, using the tools you have learned to create an authentic rapport and the confidence and willingness to listen and value the viewpoints of others can only be a positive. Very often, people feel they have to compromise when faced with making decisions, which may well be the case, but how you view this compromise makes a dramatic difference to the long-term outcome.

Summary

As a manager and a person, if you feel that you are agreeing to something out of duty or because you feel you have no choice, then sooner or later resentment and frustration will surface, that will damage not only your intended outcomes but also the relationship with the people with whom you have made the compromise.

Recognising how much you dislike this happening to you, is a great reminder in how you choose to manage the time of your staff.

This chapter has given you some strategies and tips to help you focus more clearly on how you currently spend your time and the new actions you may now wish to take.

The overarching aim in any situation is to create the maximum number of *win-win* outcomes. The following summary will highlight all tools and strategies introduced so far and a suggested resource list for further reading and information.

Example of the Time Management Matrix

Urgent	Not Urgent
I ACTIVITIES: Crises Pressing Problems Deadline-driven projects	II ACTIVITIES: Prevention, Production Capability activities Relationship building Recognising new opportunities Planning, recreation
III ACTIVITIES: Interruptions, some calls Some mail, some reports Some meetings Proximate, pressing matters Popular activities	IV ACTIVITIES: Trivia, busy work Some mail Some phone calls Time wasters Pleasant activities

Blank Time Management Matrix

Urgent	Not Urgent
I ACTIVITIES:	II ACTIVITIES:
III ACTIVITIES:	IV ACTIVITIES:

Prioritising using the Urgent v Important method

- few tasks are both urgent and important
- important tasks often only get done when they become urgent
- urgent tasks 'appear' to be important because they seem to require immediate action but some urgent tasks are not particularly important
- by confronting urgent tasks all the time, long-term goals may get put off — you are driven by the clock rather than a sense of direction.

Urgent v Important

So what makes a priority?

- urgent tasks have to be dealt with immediately
- urgent and important tasks need to be done quickly and well
- important tasks need to be given our attention.

It is therefore essential that when you think of activities to be prioritised you consider their Importance and Urgency.

The two ideas are often confused but in fact are quite different.

- Important – Something which is likely to have a major impact or long-term effect
- Urgent – Something with a short deadline

Some activities are urgent, some important, and some both important and urgent.

A Final Word and
Further Resources

My sincere hope is that you have found this book a useful guide to help you understand and know what you want to be and do to be *clearly outstanding*. As ever in life, things are a constantly moveable feast and even as this book is being written, there are yet more changes about to be made to the EYFS Curriculum and to the Ofsted Inspection guidelines and expectations.

Whatever changes may be brewing, you always have the ability to focus on what is truly important to you, both as a person and as an owner and/or manager. Being clear about what you want and then having the awareness and curiosity to stay open to whatever opportunities may be out there that will continue to shape your intentions and actions, is a tremendous attribute to have. Choosing to focus on what is right as opposed to what is wrong is also hugely important; being able to stay focused to give of your best and create and expect the best in those around you.

By consistently reviewing your practice as part of the OSCAR cycle, you will continually have the opportunity to reflect upon and review areas where you need to take ownership, examine your options more thoroughly and build upon the structure and systems, with a real sense of clarity and commitment to what you feel is right. Awareness and actions will then provide the basis for taking responsibility, communicating effectively and maintain a process of reflection to keep getting the results you want.

There are a vast range of resources, books and people you can access to help you further with your process and I have included some that I find particularly useful here.

For now, I would like to sincerely wish you luck and formally applaud you for having the passion, dedication and commitment to want to continuously strive to create the best possible outcomes for children in often very difficult circumstances and be rightly recognised as being *clearly outstanding*.

Further Resources

abcdoes.com – This is the website of Alistair Bryce Clegg, a former head teacher who now works as an Early Years consultant and is truly inspirational in helping settings create and sustain the best quality environment and practice for the nurturing and development of young minds.

The 7 Habits of Highly Effective People – Stephen R Covey

The 8th Habit — Stephen R Covey

The Leader who had no Title — Robin Sharma

The Monk who Sold his Ferrari – Robin Sharma

www.robinsharma.com

Working with Emotional Intelligence – Daniel Goleman

The Power of Empowerment – David Clutterbuck

Our Iceberg is Melting – John Kotter

Who Moved my Cheese? – Dr Spencer Johnson

www.johnadair.com

www.oscarresourcecoaching.com

Coaching for Performance – John Whitmore

The Tao of Coaching – Max Landsberg

Presenting Yourself with Impact at Work – Gill Graves

Tackling Difficult Conversations Pocketbook — Peter English

Persuasion-The Art of Influencing People – J Borg

Influence-The Psychology of Persuasion – R B Cialdini

NLP at Work – Sue Knight

NLP for Dummies —Romilla Ready and Kate Burton

CPSIA information can be obtained
at www.ICGtesting.com
Printed in the USA
LVOW13s0100211216
518114LV00013BA/1274/P